SMOKING TECHNOLOGY
OF THE ABORIGINES OF THE IROQUOIS AREA
OF NEW YORK STATE

Smoking Technology
of the Aborigines
of the Iroquois Area
of New York State

by

Edward S. Rutsch

Rutherford • Madison • Teaneck
Fairleigh Dickinson University Press

Associated University Presses, Inc.
Cranbury, New Jersey 08512

Library of Congress Cataloging in Publication Data

Rutsch, Edward S.
   Smoking technology of the aborigines of the Iroquois
area of New York State.

   Bibliography: p.
   1. Indians of North America—New York (State) —
Social life and customs. 2. Smoking. 3. Tobacco-
pipes.   4. Iroquois Indians—Social life and customs.
I. Title.
E98.T6R87   970.3   73–92558
ISBN 0–8386–7568–9

Printed in the United States of America

CONTENTS

TABLES

ACKNOWLEDGMENTS

I have studied the collections of the following institutions:

American Museum of Natural History, New York, N. Y. Courtesy Dr. M. Freed.

Brooklyn Museum of Art, Primitive Art Department, Brooklyn, N. Y.

Cayuga Museum of History and Art, Auburn, N. Y. Courtesy Professor W. K. Long.

Library of the Museum of the American Indian, New York, N. Y. Courtesy Miss Nancy Strowbridge.

Museum of the American Indian, Heye Foundation, New York, N. Y. Courtesy Dr. F. J. Dockstader.

New York State Museum, Albany, N. Y. Courtesy Dr. William A. Ritchie, Mr. Charles E. Gillette.

Rochester Museum of Arts and Sciences, Rochester, N. Y. Courtesy Dr. Charles F. Hayes.

Smithsonian Institution, Division of Cultural Anthropology, Washington, D. C. Courtesy Mr. George Metcalf.

I wish to acknowledge my indebtedness to the following individuals: Dr. Bert Salwen, Dr. Howard Winters, and Dr. Jacques Bordaz for their most valuable comments on my research; Mr. Harold Blau for his guidance and contributions in the field of Iroquois ethnology; Mr. Jerrold Stefl for his assistance on illustration methods; Miss Nancy Strowbridge for her help in library research and manuscript preparation; Mary Jane Rutsch for her editorial assistance.

Edward S. Rutsch

INTRODUCTION

Smoking technology—that is, the practice of smoke inhalation by humans, including the materials smoked, the methods and means of consumption, and the meaning of both to the participants—is a valuable and pertinent aspect of American Indian culture. Because smoking has enjoyed a many-faceted role within most Indian societies, a wealth of technical, social, and material data has been made available to the researcher. The study of smoking technology thus serves as a unique way to approach a given culture.

I shall concentrate on the smoking technology of the aborigines of the Iroquois area of New York State for several reasons: my general interest in, and propinquity to, this culture area; the characteristic distinctiveness of the material remains; and the abundance, proximity, and availability of research collections, of both artifacts and literature. For these reasons, I have been able to confine my study of the achaeological remains with the ethnohistorical data, in the belief that the light each throws upon the other is valuable to the objective researcher. My primary aim has been to construct a meaningful and analytically useful typology of the material remains (chiefly pipes) of the aboriginal smoking technology; I have also tried to present, as objectively as possible, a summation of ethnohistorical literature. My intent has been to clarify, in this manner, the role of smoking technology as I have defined it in this specific culture, and to render the information useful as an approach to the study of the entire culture, as well as a means whereby to reconstruct the culture history.

Limitation of subject allows the researcher to treat the part specifically and completely rather than the whole generally and partially. Yet, as I discuss in detail in Part II, the setting of limits in archaeology is difficult and often arbitrary. When I state that I shall study the smoking technology of the aborigines of the Iroquois area of New York State, I realize that I am superimposing, for purposes of limitation, present-day boundaries upon a geographical area inhabited through history and prehistory by constantly changing and moving cultures.

To limit my subject still further, I have chosen to focus specifically on the aborigines of that geographical area of New York State last inhabited by the Five Nations of the Iroquois Confederacy. These tribes, of course, belong to a much larger group of Iroquoian-speaking people who share many of their cultural traits (Fenton 1940:160).

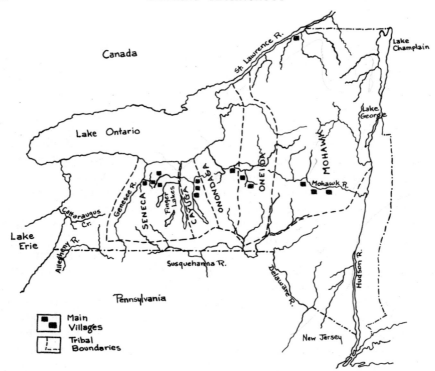

Figure 1. Location of the Five Nations from 1600 to 1650. Adapted from Ritchie 1953:Fig. 2 and Fenton 1940:Fig. 11.

Cross-cultural comparisons are included throughout, where pertinent. By "Iroquois" I shall denote members of the Iroquois Confederacy (Fig. 1); by "Iroquoian" I shall mean those people related to the Iroquois by a common language stock (Fig. 2).

Numerous problems arise, of course, when archaeological collections and possibly biased historical accounts become the analytic tools of research. I have tried to select and evaluate judiciously the literature I have cited, for, although most of the studies are extensive, many are either out of date, less than professional, or vague regarding detail. In archaeological data as well as in the ethnohistorical literature, observations may be inaccurately recorded, written in a misleading manner, or omitted altogether. I have consciously attempted to remain alert to these numerous pitfalls.

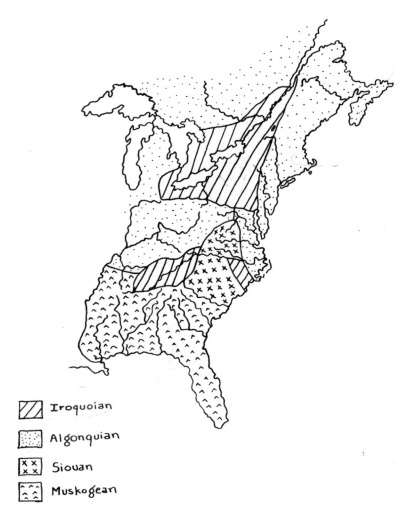

Figure 2. Location of aboriginal linguistic groups. Adapted from Driver (1964:Maps 37 and 43) and Fenton (1940:179).

SMOKING TECHNOLOGY
OF THE ABORIGINES OF THE IROQUOIS AREA
OF NEW YORK STATE

PART I.
ETHNOHISTORICAL
REPORTS

Accounts of Early Visitors

Although this study deals mainly with data and deductions of archaeologists, reports from historians and ethnographers who witnessed the aborigines' use of tobacco can broaden the prehistoric record. Post-contact Indians did grow and smoke tobacco, for most early visitors remarked on this singular trait unknown to Europeans before Columbus' time. They also described, drew, and even collected Indian pipes, thus recording more or less accurately their style, shape, and the manner in which they were used.

Apparently these Indians smoked long before the white man's arrival, for prehistoric archaeological sites have yielded pipes of similar description. I shall discuss more fully the beginnings of smoking in Part II, Archaeological Reports, but an examination of the smoking habits of the post-contact Indians is valuable to our discussion now.

The earliest account of tobacco I was able to find from the Iroquois area was Champlain's discovery in 1603 that the Indians near Quebec were cultivating the plant (West 1934:54). One of the earliest verified historical reports of tobacco use in New York appears in a translation of Juet's journal of Henry Hudson's voyage in 1609. Juet wrote that "The people have greene tobacco, and pipes, the boles whereof are made of earth, and the pipes of red copper" (Hall 1910:225). Beauchamp and others point out that although these Indians (who were probably Algonquians, eastern neighbors of the Iroquois) were very possibly smoking pipes, it seems doubtful that Juet was accurate regarding copper, for neither archaeological research nor historical reports mention the existence of pipes of that material among these Indians (Beauchamp 1902:56).

Yet, in another translation of this same journal, Juet mentions seeing copper pipes again: "They have great tobacco pipes of yellow copper. . . ." (Ritchie 1944:18). Commentators on this apparent contradiction have acknowledged the possibility that the Indians might have acquired copper sheets by trading with the French, Spanish, and Portuguese, who had frequented these coasts since the first half of the sixteenth century (Ritchie 1944:18; Parkman 1880:170–73).

Captain John Smith, exploring the upper region of the Chesapeake Bay in 1608, encountered Susquehannock Indians—Iroquoian people who lived south of the Iroquois, their traditional enemy, in Pennsylvania (Fig. 2). Smith wrote that one Indian had a "tobacco pipe three-quarters of a yard long, prettily carved with a Bird, a Deere or some such devise at the end, sufficient to beat out one's brains" (Capt. John Smith 1819:51).

Another report is that of Dutch explorer Johannes van Dyck, who lived with the Mohawks from 1634 to 1635. Van Dyck wrote that, after eating, an Indian would "produce pipe and tobacco from the pouch at his belt" (Hill 1953:9).

The Jesuit missionaries were the most literately prolific of the early visitors to the Woodland cultures of the northeastern interior. Father François du Peron described the Huron's wearing apparel as including a tobacco pouch worn behind the back. He also wrote that an accurate picture of a Huron brave would show him carrying a pipe (Thwaites 1901:Vol. 15, 155). A 1644 Jesuit account describes the installation ceremonies of an Algonquin chief, in which he was presented with tobacco and a pipe. The priest does not state whether the presentation was a gift or had ceremonial importance (Beauchamp 1907:431).

In a 1625 account of Indian life along the Hudson, Dutch historian De Laet includes a reference to stone tubes for the smoking of tobacco that were made by piercing flint, an ability he felt to be ingenious in the absence of iron tools (Ritchie 1944:19–20). Ritchie writes that "Such pipes, not however of 'flint', are an archaeological feature of the Coastal Aspect" (Ritchie 1944:20).

The first of many reports that the Iroquois in particular had witnessed calumet ceremonies[1] occurs in an account that in 1667, Iroquois chiefs passing through Miami, Mascoutens, and Kickapoo villages were received with gifts and honors of the calumet (Blair 1911:350). These tribal villages are located in the area of the Great Lakes near what is today Ohio and Michigan (Driver 1964:Map 42).

Even though it is contended that no specific ritual was associated with tobacco use at this early time, the Jesuit Le Jeune disclosed that the Hurons attributed wisdom in council and increased intelligence and abilities in political dealings to the smoking of tobacco (Thwaites 1901:Vol. 10, 219). Beauchamp reports that in 1669, Lasalle, describing a meeting with the Senecas, said that each man owned and smoked a pipe. In a meeting with Iroquois on Lake Ontario, Frontenac, another

---

1. The ceremonial smoking referred to here is the important North American Indian ritual of the calumet. This sacred shaft symbolizes either the male or the female parent, or both, or all Nature. A longitudinal chamber was later drilled through the calumet so that it could function as a pipestem, and a bowl was attached to one end to serve symbolically as an incense-burning altar. Its users regarded the pipe as the most sacred of objects, and when it was smoked, it had profound importance for everyone present. It was smoked to bind men's promises, ensuring peace and an end to all hostilities—the so-called "peace pipe." It also had the power to bring rain, ensure safe journies, and incur divine wrath on any who smoked and broke his pledge. Dances and ceremonies attending its smoking varied and can be termed generally the calumet ritual (Hewitt 1907:191–95).

French explorer, describes the council as full of pipe smokers (Beauchamp 1907:432). At the end of the seventeenth century, Father Millet
wrote that when they greeted friendly visitors, the Iroquois would
kindle a fire and each man would smoke. It seemed to him more
an act of hospitality between strangers than a ceremony (Beauchamp
1907:432).

Diffusion of Tobacco Rituals

At the beginning of the eighteenth century, the expanding contacts
of Europeans with interior tribes around the Great Lakes, eastern
plains, and the Ohio and Mississippi River basins bring reports of
the ceremonial use of the pipe. In 1712, the Minutes of the Council of
Philadelphia tell of Chief Sassoonan of the Delawares leaving with 13
braves for a visit with the Iroquois to pay their annual tribute of
32 belts of wampum. They took with them a stone calumet with a
wooden shaft decorated with feathers, given them by the Iroquois
when the Delawares had formally submitted to domination. The
calumet was to be brought and smoked at all further meetings between
the two tribes (Witthoft *et al.* 1953:91). Thus, by the early 1700's,
the Iroquois had begun to practice the calumet ritual with their
trading partners and subjugates. In 1721, however, Charlesvoix stated
that the ritual was more prevalent among the southern and western
nations than among the eastern and northern ones, implying, perhaps,
its diffusion eastward (Beauchamp 1907:432).

Others writers similarly analyze the diffusion of the calumet ritual
from the south and west to the east and north. Lafitau asserts that
the ceremonial or ritual smoking was considered remarkable by the
Woodland Indians, who regarded it as a trait associated with distant
nations (Beauchamp 1907:432). Fenton, one of the most important
modern ethnographers of the Iroquois, recounts that the early explorers first discovered ritual smoking among the peoples of the Mississippi Valley between the Great Lakes and the Saint Francis River in
Arkansas. He also asserts that similar, modern, Iroquois rituals are
analogous to the Pawnee Hako and its later variants on the northern
plains (Fenton 1953:209).

Fenton summarizes the opinion of early French explorers that the
Iroquois in the contact period did not show respect for the calumet.
He portrays the modern Iroquois eagle dance as a ritual in which

features of the former calumet rites are incorporated and thus perpetuated. He concludes his diffusion analysis by stating,

> . . . we may expect that some form of the widely distributed calumet dance diffused to the Iroquois toward the middle of the eighteenth century, either from the upper Great Lakes, from the southeast at the height of the Cherokee wars, or directly from the Pawnee, who perpetuated its most elaborate form. (Fenton 1953:12)

Fenton also mentions that the fur traders, by their movements between the western and eastern tribes, helped to spread this and other ceremonial traits (Fenton 1953:194).

Beauchamp recounts the earliest recorded use of a "ceremonial pipe" that I was able to find. The Confederacy received it from Sir William Johnson, King George's representative to the Iroquois. In his presentation, Johnson said the following:

> 'Take this pipe to your great council chamber at Onondaga. Let it hang there in view and should you be wavering in your minds at any time, take and smoke out of it, and you will recover and thinke properly.' To which the Iroquois replied, 'We assure you that we shall hang it in our council chamber and make proper use of it on all occasions.' (Beauchamp 1897:45)

This same pipe was later smoked during the conference between the Iroquois and Chief Pontiac at Oswego, New York, in July, 1766 (Beauchamp 1897:45).

The reasons for the diffusion of the calumet ritual to the Iroquois from the interior are worthy of brief consideration. This direction of diffusion might seem illogical in terms of assimilation, because, with increasing exposure to European technology, the eastern tribes would probably become technologically superior to the more primitive inland tribes who could offer them few innovations.

George T. Hunt analyzes this phenomenon in his illuminating book, *The Wars of the Iroquois* (1940), when he treats the puzzling problem of why the Confederacy could, and in a short time did, gain supremacy over vast areas and people. After discussing and refuting the traditional theories, Hunt presents the thesis that expansion resulted from the Iroquois' economic need to remain a partner in the European fur trade. As the Five Nations depleted the fur-bearing animals in their own territory, trade moved gradually westward toward more prolific trapping grounds. The Iroquois, who were situated between the coastal Europeans and the inland Indians, could control the trade routes (and thus the trade itself, of course) from their middle-man position. Understandably, the inland tribes were eager to sell their furs directly to the Europeans for greater profit. In the subsequent struggle for domination, the Iroquois subdued one tribe after another, forcing each to become economically dependent upon the Confederacy (Hunt 1940:11–12).

However, the historian Trelease maintains that "Iroquois power depended on several factors, no one of which is sufficient to explain the phenomenon by itself" (Trelease 1960:24). The Confederacy protected any raiding member nation from the rear, and thus formed a strong base for military operations. The Dutch and English supplied the Iroquois with arms to maintain a buffer zone between themselves and the French and their tribal allies. The rapid ascent to power of the Iroquois Confederacy, then, resulted from political, geographical, and miltary, as well as economic, factors.

Thus, the Iroquois, moving westward on trading and warring expeditions, became acquainted with western customs and rituals. They might have adopted the calumet ritual initially to ensure a peaceful trading atmosphere. It would then appear that the returning traders brought these ceremonies and accoutrements home with them, where they were eventually adopted.

The ethologist Konrad Lorenz has suggested a psychological explanation for the peaceful-meeting context of the calumet ritual. He considers it to function as a "displacement activity" (Lorenz 1966:73–74), which became an established ritual. Without judging this interpretation, we can note that the established ritual did, indeed, serve to reduce aggression.

Tobacco in Indian Mythology

Our discussion of ethnographic reports of tobacco use among the tribes in question will perhaps be more meaningful if we first examine at least one Indian myth concerning the origin of the plant. A present-day former teacher of the Iroquois (Akweks 1951) relates that in a camp on the Ohio River, a canoe full of medicine people[2] approached

---

2. Medicine people and supernatural creatures in conflict with the Iroquois frequently appear in other Iroquois origin myths. In these fables, the Great Maker or Supreme Deity engages in a series of contests with a Shagodjiowen gowa, a being who has lived with uncontested authority among the creatures of the Great Maker's world so long that he feels equal or superior to the deity. The Great Maker easily wins the encounters and punishes the Shagodjiowen gowa by dropping him on, or causing him to collide with, a mountain. The impact crushes his face and body, leaving him alive but forever twisted and gnomelike (Keppler 1941:17).

the shore. The members of the encampment crowded toward the bank, attracted by the singing and peculiar appearance of these creatures. As the excitement continued, a voice from the canoe warned the Indians to leave the bank or suffer misfortune. Most, awed by what they had seen and heard, returned to their homes for safety. The braver, or more foolhardy, few who remained were found dead when later the others returned to the scene of the apparition.

A war party set out immediately in canoes to avenge the murders. The Indians sighted the medicine people's canoe, and, upon approaching it, found two of the creatures asleep in its bottom. A mysterious voice told them that if they killed the creatures they would obtain a great blessing for mankind. One warrior was elected to awaken and taunt the creatures. Enraged, they chased him into the village council house where the others ambushed and killed them, burning their bodies in the council-house fire. It was from this fire place that the first tobacco plant grew, and, after it had matured, the same mysterious voice instructed the Indians in its use.

Accounts of Later Observers

In accounts of the calumet ritual's diffusion, we have already discussed the beginnings of tobacco as a ceremonial adjunct. Nineteenth- and twentieth-century ethnographers have written a great deal more on the significance of tobacco in this and other rituals. In my analysis of their work, I shall cite examples of this usage rather than attempt to summarize all the field work that has been done.

Ceremonial and Magical Uses of Tobacco

We should begin our discussion with the note that the Indians have distinguished between the ceremonial value of the original "true tobacco" and that of the variety introduced by the Europeans. "True tobacco" is an Indian appellation for the plant originally grown by the aboriginal people of this area, generally assumed to be *Nicotiana rustica* rather than *Nicotiana tabacum*, imported from Central and South America by European cultivators (Arents 1939:4). Neither species is native to North America.

Many ethnographers have commented on this distinction. De Cost Smith mentions that the Indians used only *N. rustica* in their ceremonies. To ensure good hunting, Indians smoked only true tobacco on their hunting trips (De Cost Smith 1889B:282). Alanson Skinner noted that Senecas valued this variety more highly than the commercial types because it was indispensable to their rites and ceremonies; the barter value for one teaspoon of native tobacco was an entire plug of the European-introduced variety (Skinner 1925:129). James Mooney and Frans Olbrechts found that the Cherokee medicine men grew *N. rustica* for ritual and medicinal purposes as late as the 1930's (Mooney and Olbrechts, 1932:91), and Harold Blau, ethnographer of the Onondaga, reports that true tobacco is still grown on the Onondaga Reservation at Nedro for ceremonial purposes (Blau, personal communication, 1966).

Several interesting features of the ritual use of tobacco are present in one record of an eagle dance ritual at the Cold Spring Reservation in Allegany County (Fenton 1953:185). The ceremony began with the thanksgiving prayer, which included special thanks for the true tobacco. Immediately after this prayer, Wood Eater, the Indian who delivered that incantation, took a plate of tobacco to a fire in the kitchen of the Indian dwelling and prayed again, very softly. As he did so, he placed pinches of tobacco in the flames[3] (Fenton 1953:15). When asked why he prayed so inaudibly, he replied that tobacco offering magnified communication between man and the Dew Eagle Spirit. He added that out of respect, a man should speak softly to the Spirit so as to seem neither scolding nor demanding in manner. I interpret the translation of the prayer (Fenton 1953:146) to mean that the tobacco is both a ritual gift and a ritual payment by which man fulfills his obligation to the Eagle Spirit.

During the eagle dance ritual, tobacco is similarly burned for the song, the drum, the fan, and the rattles. At the end of these offerings, the singer chants,

It is fulfilled
So it is finished.

Then, the plate with the remaining tobacco is placed on the floor, and each man who wishes fills his pipe and smokes (Fenton 1953:15–16).

Other accounts written since the beginning of the nineteenth century mention the Iroquois' ritual use of tobacco. Hale witnessed a burning-of-the-white-dog ceremony on an Iroquois reservation in Canada.

As the fire consumed the body, handfuls of finely cut tobacco were cast, from time to time, as incense into the flames. (Hale 1885:7)

---

3. Other ethnographers mention that northeastern Indians make similar ritual tobacco gifts to the spirits in which they burn tobacco pinch by pinch. Harrington writes that the Delaware begin to pray with the twelfth pinch (Harrington 1965:19).

De Cost Smith reported a visitation by the masked society. By legend, the masked demon Ho^n-do'-I, to get a gift of tobacco, jumped into the council-house fire, kicking it apart until he was promised and given his desire. Smith writes that the leader of the group assumes the role of Ho^n-do'-I by rushing at the fire. He is then held or thrown back by the council members who promise him tobacco. In the ritual following, tobacco is burned in small pinches. Afterward, all that is left is given to the Indian representing the spirit (De Cost Smith 1889A:227).

In his comments on Indian masks, Joseph Keppler mentions the use of "sacred tobacco" several times in relation to these venerated objects. Tobacco is burned at the base of the tree before a mask is cut into it. The Tree Spirit is thus appeased and asks that its life spirit be continued in the mask to be "carved and hewn from its loins," and the tree trunk is "propitiated with the incense of the sacred tobacco." Furthermore, bags of sacred tobacco are tied to masks to keep them content (Fig. 3). Should a mask "sweat"—that is, become "sick" according to

Figure 3. Onondaga medicine mask of wood, showing cloth bag filled with sacred tobacco hanging from its nose. Drawn from original in the Heye Foundation Museum of the American Indian, Catalog No. 8/7845. It was carved by Elyjah Hill on the Onondaga Reservation in New York, and collected by Joseph Keppler and George Heye.

Keppler—or be treated improperly, sacred tobacco would be burned to soothe and heal the trouble. The Indians would also burn tobacco to the harvest mask in a drought, imploring it to intercede with the Spirit of Thunder, the Bringer of Rain, or the Sky Eagle, which could let water fall from its feathers in life-giving dew (Keppler 1941:24–39).

De Cost Smith also mentions masks "sweating." When he was obtaining a false face in the 1880's, an Indian asked him for tobacco. When Smith gave it to him, he burned half, pinch by pinch, and tied the rest in a cloth bag and hung it from the mask. The tribesman warned Smith that if he did not repeat this process every three months, the mask would bring "frights and illnesses" upon him for depriving it of "feasts and dances" (De Cost Smith 1888:192–93).

Blau has witnessed several other instances of the ceremonial use of tobacco as propitiation. True tobacco is hung on a mask while more is burned to appease the spirit before it is called upon to heal. Blau concurs that certain Onondaga masks "sweat" occasionally, having observed this moisture on these masks while others have remained dry. The Indians interpret this phenomenon to be the mask's indication or prediction that it will be needed to cure a future illness of some member of the family that houses it (Blau, personal communication, 1966).

Blau's translation of the Onondaga's mid-winter rites of 1962 provides a fine illustration of the propitiative qualities attributed to ritual tobacco. After the tobacco and the white-dog symbol are cast into the fire, the chief prays, chanting,

> We send these goods to thee Creator, to prove our words are true. Listen to the pleas of thy people who beseech thee for beneficial things and for wisdom. Give us the power to maintain your ceremonies faithfully. We thank thee for preserving all things. (Blau 1964:100)

Prayers during which tobacco is burned are usually offered in propitiation; those during which t. bacco is not burned are generally offered in thanksgiving (Blau, personal communication, 1966).

Beauchamp writes of a nonritual use of tobacco as a propitiate. After crossing a lake in stormy weather accompanied by the Indian Te kan a di e, he says that the Iroquois solemnly threw tobacco into the water to appease the Storm Spirit (Beauchamp 1889:234).

In 1925, along with observations that the Senecas used true tobacco as a form of exchange, gambling with small packets valued at about ten cents each, Skinner found that *N. rustica* was important in sorcery. Senecas believe that a member of the tobacco society can burn this variety and, by pronouncing the proper incantation, cause his victim's mouth to become drawn up like a distorted mask. They also believe that burning tobacco can cause lightning when they simultaneously implore Heno, the Thunder Being. If a man's wife runs away, her husband need only smoke one bowl of this tobacco in her direction and she will be impelled to return (Skinner 1925:129–30).

Nicotiana rustica's extensive ritualistic properties are evident in the cultivation practices prescribed for medicinal plants. Tobacco was

spread near growing plants that would later be gathered to make medicine. The Indians left a small offering of tobacco near the first plant
of the particular medicine variety, which remained untouched when
the other plants were harvested. This offering ensured that plants of
this species would continue to grow in the future (Beauchamp
1889:234).

Medicinal Uses of Tobacco

Tobacco was also used for medicinal purposes. Whenever a man
bled excessively—a so-called "red" disease—he could be cured if another
man gave him tobacco, a feast of corn meal mush, and some gravy
(De Cost Smith 1889A:279). Fenton reports that *N. rustica* is still
used as a remedy in "blood" diseases (Fenton 1942:524). In another
account, an Iroquois burned tobacco and then rubbed the ashes on the
heads of people in a large crowd to heal an indeterminable number of
ills (Kell 1965:100). Onondagas are reported to cure facial inflamma-
tions with a wad of chewed tobacco applied as a poultice (Beauchamp
1889:234).

Cultivation of Tobacco Plants

Seneca chief Esquire Johnson reportedly told Mrs. Asher Johnson,
a missionary who related the story to ethnographers, that cultivated
plants grew from the Earth Mother's body: squash from her navel;
beans from above her feet; tobacco from above her head. "Thus," he
added, "it soothes the mind and sobers the thought" (Setchell
1921:402).

In his study of aboriginal pipes published in 1905, A. F. Berlin notes
that *N. rustica* was "cultivated sparingly" by Onondagas in New York,
who called it "oyenkwa honne," or real tobacco[4] (Berlin 1905:110).
As late as 1921, W. A. Setchell reported that a chief named Cornplanter
sent him seeds of *N. rustica* that he and scientists at the Brooklyn
Botanical Gardens in New York City were able to propagate success-
fully (Setchell 1921:402). I have already mentioned Blau's statement
that the traditional tobacco is still used in Onondaga ceremonies and

---

4. The Iroquois had several other names for tobacco: the Mohawks and Cayugas called
it "oyeang wa"; the Senecas called it "oyanquva" (Wiener 1925:313).

cultivated specifically for this purpose on the reservation near Syracuse, New York (Blau, personal communication, 1966).

Indeed, the cultivation process itself reflects the Indians' great respect for this particular crop. Ralph Linton has summarized early cultivation accounts.[5] Tobacco was not grown with other crops for it was believed to be injurious to them. It was usually cultivated by men (Linton 1924:3), a particularly interesting fact because crop cultivation among the Iroquois was woman's work (Drumm 1962:2). A certain Milford Chandler informed Linton that the Cayugas grew tobacco annually in permanent beds, uncultivated but occasionally lightly manured. As the untended plants matured, the Indians gathered only the leaves, allowing the stems and seeds to propagate new plants (Linton 1924:3).

In 1925, Skinner visited the Senecas to obtain tobacco plants for a proposed Indian garden to be located at the Research Annex of the Museum of the American Indian in New York City. The Indians claimed no knowledge of their people's cultivating tobacco. They said the seeds were simply thrown by the door to survive or perish by chance (Skinner 1925:128). Linton also mentions the Senecas, who told him they simply scattered the seeds on the ground because their religion prohibited cultivation of the tobacco plant (Linton 1924:3).

Tobacco leaves were picked when they attained a size roughly double the area formed when a man joined his right and left thumbs and his right and left forefingers and held his hands in an outstretched position. They were collected only as a thunderstorm approached, for tobacco so harvested was said to curl and burn slowly, carrying the smoker's or burner's message directly to the spirits. Tobacco not picked in this prestorm period supposedly burned too fast and rose in a manner unacceptable to the spirits (Skinner 1925:128).

Botanical Discussion of Tobacco

Nicotiana rustica (Fig. 4) is described as clammy and hairy, about three feet tall, with ovate or roundish ovate leaves set alternately along the plant stem. Its leaves, although smaller and coarser than those of

---

5. Unfortunately, Linton's work on tobacco is inadequately documented. Nevertheless, much of his information is relevant and enlightening; therefore, I feel it should be mentioned.

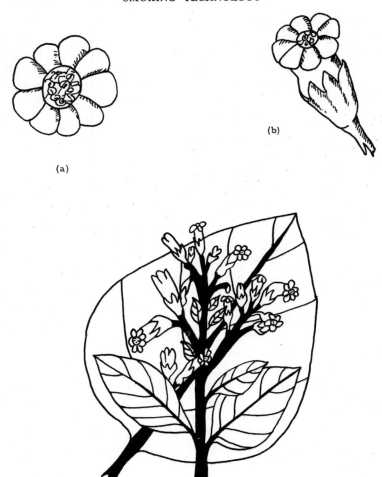

(a)

(b)

(c)

Figure 4. Nicotiana rustica. (a) **Flower seen from above. (b) Side view of flower. (Illustrations from Hegi n.d.:2611, No. 233.) (c) Composite drawing of plant against an enlarged leaf. (Illustration from Gleason 1952:205.)**

N. tabacum, grow as much as one foot long. The flower is yellow or yellowish green, in thyrises or panicles, day opening, self-fertilizing, and approximately three-quarters of an inch long (Chittenden 1956: 1370).

In 1952, H. A. Gleason wrote that *N. rustica* was "at present rare" in the northeastern United States, possibly extinct, and last reported growing along roadsides in Indian settlements of western New York.

He pointed out that the species grows wild in Peru but not in New York State, implying that its presence there resulted from its introduction into the area and its continued cultivation (Gleason 1952:204). Ethnobotanist R. A. Yarnell concurs with this hypothesis, observing that *N. rustica* is not native to the eastern United States and therefore must have been introduced from South America. That today it is found occasionally growing untended in the area he attributes to its acclimatization by continued cultivation (Yarnell 1964:145).

Smoking Materials and Mixtures

The grown, gathered, and cured crop was generally mixed with other materials before it was smoked. The methods and materials of mixing were varied; several appear in the following list. Dogwood (*Cornus sericea*) was a popular addition to tobacco and the Indian name for the resulting mixture, "kinnikinnick" (or "that which is mixed," from the Cree and Chippewa dialects of the Algonquian language stock), came to be used generally for tobacco mixtures made by all the northeastern Indians (Ritzenthaler 1955:14), although Fenton reports that kinnikinnick is the Iroquois name for *Cornus amomum* used as an emetic (Fenton 1942:524). The amount of the material in the mixture other than tobacco varied a good deal, although R. E. Ritzenthaler has gone so far as to say "whatever plant material was used, it usually dominated the final mixture which generally contained about one-third tobacco" (Ritzenthaler 1955:15).

Various representative mixtures appear in the following list.[6]

1. Kinnikinnick: a mixture of tobacco and *C. sericea*, a type of dogwood shrub.
2. Pl'likinick (*Cornus stolonifera*): red osier dogwood; mixed with tobacco.
3. *Viburnum acerifolium*: arrow root (also called maple leaved *Viburnum* and dockmackie); prepared by drying the bark and rubbing it between the hands; smoked as a tobacco substitute.
4. *Rhus glabra*: sumac; mixed equally with tobacco.
5. *Kalmia latifolia*: laurel (also called spoonwood and calicobush); the dried leaf was mixed with tobacco.

---

6. References for 1–15 are from Philhower 1934:4. The reference for 16 is Linton 1924:7. General references include: Bailey 1935; Murphy 1959; Peattie 1950; Dana 1910.

6. *Carpinas carolinoana*: iron wood; the dried leaf was mixed with tobacco.
7. Waahoo (*Euonymus atropureus*) : burning bush; a tobacco substitute.
8. *Polycodium stamineum*: squaw huckleberry (also called *Vaccinium stamineum*) ; the leaf and bark were smoked.
9. *Lobelia inflata*: Indian tobacco; included here more because of its name than its use, although there is a report that when the dry leaves are smoked, they impart a tobacco taste.
10. *Datura stramonium*: Jamestown weed (also called thorn apple and white man's plant by the Indians) ; mixed with tobacco for a lethargic or narcotic effect on the mind.
11. *Betula lenta*: black birch; used in small amounts to improve flavor.
12. *Prunus serotina*: cherry bark; used to improve flavor.
13. *Zea saccharata*: Indian maize; tradition says the silk was smoked, but no confirmed report exists.
14. *Verbascum*: mullein, a figwort; mixed with tobacco for musky flavor.
15. Muskrat glands or oil: used for aroma.
16. Animal oil or rendered fat: used to bind the dust.

How each or any of the tribes in the Iroquois area of New York made and used smoking materials and mixtures is conjectural, but we can assume that they probably did use some or all of the preceding mixtures. Several reasons for using mixtures are covered by this list. Another probable motivation could be the economic factor that mixing stretched the valuable and often limited tobacco supply (Ritzenthaler 1955:15) . It is known that tobacco was probably scarce in some areas. The Tionontati tribe, living in the area above Lake Ontario, were named the Petuns—literally, "the Tobaccos"—by the French, because they grew a surplus tobacco crop for trade with other tribes (Linton 1924:7) .

As the preceding list indicates, smoking mixtures did not necessarily include tobacco as a constituent. Yarnell notes that the Woodland Indians of the Great Lakes smoked tobaccoless mixtures of at least 23 known plants. Eleven of these served the function of attracting deer, for the Indians discovered that the smell produced a scent that acted as a lure. An additional 12 plants either functioned as tobacco substitutes or were actually preferred to tobacco (Yarnell 1964:180) . This variance in smoking materials has led Yarnell to warn us that to assume a given pipe, whether historic or prehistoric, was used to smoke tobacco is potentially invalid (Yarnell 1964:145) .

Chemical analysis of pipe dottle and such residues may become a useful tool in the attempt to determine the nature of the smoking materials and mixtures used by the Indian. The first of these analyses was published in 1922 and was performed on "dottle" and "cake" from three Basket Maker pipes of the southwestern United States. These tests were inconclusive in detecting nicotine (Dixon and Stetson 1922:245).

More recent, but as yet unpublished, analyses of pipe residues for lithium, an element distinctively present in tobacco ash, may prove effective. The details and results of the experimentation are not yet complete, but hopefully they will provide not only conclusive answers to the question but also a process by which we can diagnose the presence of tobacco (Winters, personal communication, 1966–67; Wittry, personal communication, 1967).

PART II.
ARCHAEOLOGICAL REPORTS

Research Problems

In extending my study beyond the written record of ethnohistory to encompass the material evidence discovered and recorded by archaeologists, I have encountered numerous problems that may be considered typical for this type of research. In my introduction, I have commented on the problems related to the availability and reliability of the material culture remains and data concerning them. The researcher also must take into account that the ability to read the record of the soil is not static. The tools of the science have become more numerous and complex and are handled differently by innumerable archaeologists of various backgrounds and abilities. Then, too, archaeology has both benefited and suffered from a recent growth of public interest, for although research funds are more readily available in increasing amounts, pothunters—the bane of amateur and professional alike, who disturb the archaeological record indiscriminately and irreparably—have also multiplied.

All these factors complicate the researcher's task; however, once he has acknowledged and is wary of their presence, another type of problem arises. Two such dilemmas need explanation here: geographical limitation and chronological definition.

Geographical Limitation

In my introductory remarks at the beginning of this work, I defined my topic as the smoking technology of the aborigines of that area of New York State last inhabited by the Five Nations of the Iroquois Confederacy. I did so realizing that today's political boundaries have little bearing on the historic Indian population and none at all, of course, on the prehistoric tribes. The aborigines moved their habitations often: in the Archaic Period, they continually sought new hunting, fishing, and gathering sites; in the Woodland Period, they searched for new areas with arable soil and adequate firewood supplies (Fenton 1940:167; Wray and Schoff 1953:53–54; Ritchie 1958:108). An ethnohistorical observation of the animosity between Iroquoian and Algonquian peoples (Hunt 1940; and others) indicates the possibility that the conflict may also have been of an undeterminably long prehistoric origin. If this conjecture is true (and, of course, we shall never be certain), untold prehistoric population shifts may have resulted from

37

these intercultural conflicts. Therefore, although I concentrate on this generally defined area, I cannot ignore pertinent archaeological data from other sections of New York, or, indeed, from the entire Northeast.

Ritchie has recently set the geographical guidelines for New York State archaeology. He subdivides the state into five subcultural areas (Ritchie 1965:Fig. 4, 38–39), each of which apparently exhibits a homogeneity of archaeological remains and constitutes one major watershed or drainage system (Ritchie 1965:xx). Ritchie admits that his subareas are "somewhat arbitrary" but qualifies this statement by adding that in each section "the prehistoric course of events seems to have been more consistent than was the case between any two separate sections" (Ritchie 1965:xx).

To follow Ritchie's system and to use his terminology are not only convenient for the writer, but also helpful to the reader who may have to correlate information from various sources in the quickest and most efficient manner possible. A generally accepted nomenclature and accurate terminology facilitate his job. For these reasons, then, I shall relate the artifacts discussed to these specific subareas. Figure 5 is my rendition of Ritchie's map; I have included county boundaries

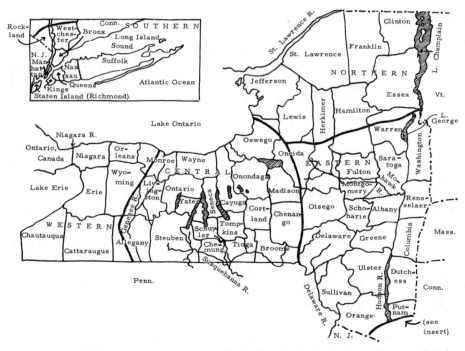

Figure 5. Subcultural areas of New York State. Adapted from Ritchie 1965:Figs. 3 and 4. County boundaries have been added to facilitate reference.

Figure 6. **Cultural areas of southern Ontario, Canada. Dashed lines indicate tribal boundaries of areas having artifacts similar to those from the Iroquois area of New York. Counties are included for reference. Adapted from Rand McNally 1966:72; tribal data from Fenton 1940:Fig. 11, 178.**

to facilitate reference. Figure 6 illustrates the cultural areas of Ontario, Canada, artifacts from which have been useful to my discussion.

Chronological Definition

The problem presented by chronological definition—that is, the determination and use of valid and workable criteria for studying material culture remains relative to each other in a time sequence—cannot be completely divorced from the difficulties we have encountered in geographical limitation. Stratigraphy can confirm, for example, that artifacts from a given site do not necessarily reveal the gradual development of only one group of aborigines. A particularly good habitation site may have been used by various cultures at various times and may even have been the motive for intercultural conflict. It is difficult, then, to establish a New York State chronology when intrusions of artifacts evidently indicate migrations of peoples to and from this given locale.

Other problems of chronology, just as obvious, arise to plague the researcher; perhaps the greatest impediment, however, is the fact that any archaeological chronology is necessarily based on what we know— that is, what we have unearthed. We cannot know what remains to be discovered. We can never even be sure that we are saving and examining the correct remains. Carbon dating and pollen analysis have already proved that charcoal and jars of soil from site levels may be as important as the corresponding boxes of artifacts.

However, I shall not attempt to analyze all the factors that make compilation of such a chronology an awesome task, for, once again, we find that Ritchie has recently published a workable, up-to-date chronology (Ritchie 1965:Fig. 1, xviii–ixx), in which he has considered and allowed for many of the problems I have just stated. For example, he warns that acceptance of his scheme should be predicated on realization that it is an archaeological conclusion based on deductions from existing material (Ritchie 1965:xvii).

For the same reasons, then, that I elected to use Ritchie's subcultural-area scheme, I shall relate the artifacts I shall discuss to his chronology, with certain qualifications (Table 1). I have used only two of Ritchie's headings: Stage; Culture or Tradition. I have not adopted his Phase classification because I found it impossible to make distinctions at this fine a level. I have also modified Ritchie's "Adena" to "Early Woodland," inasmuch as there exists some doubt regarding the interaction (if any) and/or the influence (if any) the Adena Culture in Ohio had with or exerted upon the aborigines of the Iroquois area (Winters, personal communication, 1967; Griffin 1961:572).

Whereas the sites I have studied are not necessarily those used by Ritchie when he compiled his table, they have all been identified in the literature. In Table 2, I have cited them alphabetically and have included bibliographical references and geographical locations, as accurately as possible, for quick cross reference.

TABLE 1. Sites in the Iroquois Area Attributable to Culture and Subarea*

Stage	Culture or Tradition		Subcultural Areas†			
			W	C	N	E
LATE WOODLAND	IROQUOIAN	Historic	Buffam Street Goodyear Green Lake Orchard Kienuka Oakfield Ripley Shelby	Adams Center Big Salmon Creek Big Tree Farm Boughton Hill Canawaugus Dann Dutch Hollow East Cayuga Factory Hollow Fleming Genoa Great Gully McClintock Burial 1 Oakwood Orringh Stone Tavern Rochester Junction Sackett Scipioville, Lot 26	Ellisburg Marsh Watertown	Oak Hill 2 Oak Hill 3 Oak Hill 7 Sand Hill 1 Weaver Lake
		?	Burning Springs Ellington Earthwork 1 McCullough Earthwork	Cornish Hopewell Hummel Powerhouse Raine's Farm	Calcium Calligan Farm Ellisburg Morse Farm Rutland Hills Talcott Farm Theresa	Deowongo Island Dewandalaer El Rancho England's Woods Galligan Jay Nellis Swart-Farley
		Prehistoric	Double Wall Fort Sheridan Earthwork Silverheels Westfield	Aurora Locke Reed Fort	Black River Putnam Rocky Rift	South Cruger Island Weaver Lake

* The sites listed are those from which I have identified artifacts and which the literature attributes to given cultures and areas. Sites either partially or totally unidentifiable, archaeologically and/or geographically, do not appear in Tables 1 and 2 but may be mentioned in the discussion of the types for emphasis or illustration. The Southern Subarea has been omitted in Tables 1 and 2 because it is outside the Iroquois area; however, it is included in the data evaluations (see Tables 4 and 5).

† The Western, Central, Northern, and Eastern Subareas are represented by W, C, N, and E.

TABLE 1 (cont.)

| Stage | Culture or Tradition | Subcultural Areas | | | |
		W	C	N	E
MIDDLE WOODLAND	OWASCO	Kiantone	Bainbridge Canandaigua Castle Creek Jack's Reef Levanna Owasco Lake Wickham Point Willow Point Willow Tree	Phelp's Farm St. Lawrence	Enders Snell
MIDDLE WOODLAND	POINT PENINSULA	Newton Hill	Big Tree Farm Jack's Reef Kipp Island Sea Breeze Squawkie Hill Wickham Point Williams Mound Wray	Pt. Peninsula Red Lake	River Turnbull
EARLY WOODLAND	EARLY WOODLAND		Amber Camillus Cuylerville Hemlock Lake Hubbardsville Kashong Kipp Island Vine Valley Walsh	Long Sault Island	Bradt East Branch Fish Creek Hoffmans Palatine Bridge Scotia Stillwater Toll-Clute

TABLE 2

Alphabetical List of Sites with Location and Bibliographical Data

Site	Location*	County	Culture or Tradition	Area†	Bibliographical Data
Adams Center	Adams Center	Livingston	Hist. Iroquoian	C	Wray 1956B:8; Lenig 1965:8
Amber	Otisco Lake	Onondaga	Early Woodland	C	Ritchie 1937:186
Aurora	Cayuga Lake	Cayuga	Prehist. Iroquoian	C	Skinner 1921:46
Bainbridge	Bainbridge	Chenango	Owasco	C	Ritchie 1944:29; Ritchie and MacNeish 1949:Fig. 43; Ritchie 1953:3; Yarnell 1964:124
Bell-Philhower	Montague	Sussex Co., N. J.	Owasco and Iroquoian	—	Ritchie 1965:299
Big Salmon Creek	Venice Center	Cayuga	Hist. Iroquoian	C	Skinner 1921:53
Big Tree Farm**	Geneseo	Livingston	Pt. Peninsula	C	Ritchie 1938:119–20; Hayes 1965:7
Black River	Black River	Jefferson	Hist. Iroquoian	N	Skinner 1921:121
Boughton Hill	Victor	Ontario	Prehist. Iroquoian	C	Wray and Graham 1966
Bradt	near Scotia	Schenectady	Hist. Iroquoian	E	Ritchie 1944:197
Buffam Street	Buffalo	Erie	Early Woodland	W	White 1961:58
Burning Springs	Perrysburg	Cattaraugus	Hist. Iroquoian	W	Guthe 1958:41
Calcium	Calcium	Jefferson	Iroquoian	N	Skinner 1921:122
Calligan Farm	Black River	Jefferson	Iroquoian	N	Skinner 1921:155
Camillus	—	Onondaga	Iroquoian	C	Beauchamp 1897:53
Canandaigua	Sackett	Ontario	Early Woodland; Owasco	C	Ritchie 1953:3; Hayes 1965:9
Canawaugus	Caladonia	Livingston	Hist. Iroquoian	C	Hayes 1965:4; Ritchie 1936:4
Castle Creek	Castle Creek	Broome	Owasco	C	Ritchie 1953:3; Crane 1956:667; Guthe 1958:19; Yarnell 1964:124

* Often to nearest town or identifiable map point.

† As in Table 1, Western, Central, Northern, and Eastern Subareas are denoted by W, C, N, and E.

** Also known as the Geneseo Mound site or the Wadsworth site (see references).

TABLE 2 (cont.)

Site	Location*	County	Culture or Tradition	Area†	Bibliographical Data
Cornish	West Bloomfield	Ontario	Iroquoian	C	Lenig 1965:97
Cuylerville	Leicester	Livingston	Early Woodland	C	Ritchie and Dragoo 1960:29
Dann	Genessee River Valley	Monroe	Hist. Iroquoian	C	Wray and Schoff 1953:58
Deowongo Island	Canadarago Lake	Otsego	Iroquoian	E	Ritchie 1952:9 Lenig 1965:36
Dewandalaer	Canajoharie	Montgomery	Iroquoian	E	Lenig 1965:19
Double Wall Fort	Perrysburg	Cattaraugus	Prehist. Iroquoian	W	Guthe 1958:48
Dutch Hollow	Avon	Livingston	Hist. Iroquoian	C	Ritchie 1954 Wray 1956B:8 Lenig 1965:97
East Branch	East Branch	Delaware	Early Woodland	E	Ritchie and Dragoo 1960:39
East Cayuga	Fleming	Cayuga	Hist. Iroquoian	C	Skinner 1921:49
El Rancho	Palatine Bridge	Montgomery	Iroquoian	E	Lenig 1965:22
Ellington Earthwork 1	Ellington	Chautauqua	Iroquoian	W	Guthe 1958:46
Ellisburg	Roberts Corners	Jefferson	Iroquoian Hist. Iroquoian	N	Yarnell 1964:124 Parker 1922:579
Enders	Esperance	Schenectady	Owasco	E	Ritchie 1953:3
England's Woods	Fonda	Montgomery	Iroquoian	E	Lenig 1965:30
Factory Hollow	West Bloomfield	Ontario	Hist. Iroquoian	C	Parker 1922:657 Wray 1956B:8
Fish Creek	NW of Mechanicville	Saratoga	Early Woodland	E	Ritchie and Dragoo 1960:Fig. 1
Fleming	Fleming	Cayuga	Hist. Iroquoian	C	Skinner 1921:49 Parker 1922:505
Galligan	Fort Plain	Montgomery	Iroquoian	E	Lenig 1965:33
Genoa	Genoa	Cayuga	Hist. Iroquoian	C	Skinner 1921:54
Goodyear	Elma	Erie	Hist. Iroquoian	W	White 1961:61
Great Gully	Ledyard, Scipio	Cayuga	Hist. Iroquoian	C	Skinner 1921:55 Fenton 1940:223
Green Lake Orchard	Orchard Park	Erie	Hist. Iroquoian	W	White 1961:62
Hemlock Lake	near Conesus	Livingston	Early Woodland	C	Ritchie and Dragoo 1960:Fig. 1

TABLE 2 (cont.)

Site	Location*	County	Culture or Tradition	Area†	Bibliographical Data
Hoffmans	Hoffmans	Schenectady	Early Woodland	E	Ritchie 1937:186
Hopewell	Canandaigua	Ontario	Iroquoian	C	Parker 1922:661
Hubbardsville	Hubbardsville	Madison	Early Woodland	C	Ritchie and Dragoo 1960:Map 10
Hummel	Bristol Hills	Livingston	Iroquoian	C	White 1956:14
Jack's Reef	W of Iona	Onondaga	Pt. Peninsula Owasco	C	Ritchie 1953:3
Jay Nellis	Nelliston	Montgomery	Iroquoian	E	Lenig 1965:28
Kashong	Seneca Lake	Ontario	Early Woodland	C	Ritchie and Dragoo 1960:Map 11
Kiantone	Conewango Creek	Chautauqua	Owasco	W	Guthe 1958:19
Kienuka	Lewiston	Niagara	Hist. Iroquoian	W	White 1961:54
Kipp Island	Montezuma	Seneca	Early Woodland Pt. Peninsula	C	Ritchie and Dragoo 1960:37 Ritchie 1965:Fig. 1
Levanna	Cayuga Lake	Cayuga	Owasco	C	Skinner 1921:42
Locke	Locke	Cayuga	Prehist. Iroquoian	C	Ritchie and Dragoo 1960:41
Long Sault Island	Massena	St. Lawrence	Early Woodland	N	
McCullough Earthwork	Gerry	Chautauqua	Iroquoian	W	Guthe 1958:43 Yarnell 1964:124
McClintock Burial 1	East Bloomfield	Ontario	Hist. Iroquoian	C	Hoffman 1956:3
Marsh	Watertown	Jefferson	Hist. Iroquoian	N	Wray 1956B:8
Morse Farm	Watertown	Jefferson	Iroquoian	N	Rochester Museum notes
Newton Hill	Irving	Chautauqua	Pt. Peninsula	W	Guthe 1958:18
Oakfield	Oakfield	Genesee	Hist. Iroquoian	W	White 1961:52
Oak Hill 2, 3, 7	Fort Plain	Montgomery	Hist. Iroquoian	E	Lenig 1965:24–28
Oakwood	Union Springs	Cayuga	Hist. Iroquoian	C	Skinner 1921:49
Orringh Stone Tavern	Brighton	Monroe	Hist. Iroquoian	C	Hayes 1965:2
Owasco Lake	Auburn	Cayuga	Owasco	C	Ritchie 1953:3 Yarnell 1964:124
Palatine Bridge	Palatine Bridge	Montgomery	Early Woodland	E	Ritchie 1937:186
Phelp's Farm	Adams	Jefferson	Owasco	N	Rochester Museum notes
Point Peninsula	Point Peninsula	Jefferson	Pt. Peninsula	C	Ritchie 1953:3
Powerhouse	Lima	Livingston	Iroquoian	C	Parker 1922:596
Putnam	Black River	Jefferson	Prehist. Iroquoian	N	Skinner 1921:173
Raine's Farm	East Bloomfield	Ontario	Iroquoian	C	Parker 1922:665

TABLE 2 (cont.)

Site	Location*	County	Culture or Tradition	Area†	Bibliographical Data
Red Lake		Jefferson	Pt. Peninsula	N	Ritchie 1955:66
Reed Fort	Richmond Mills	Ontario	Prehist. Iroquoian	C	White 1956:14
Ripley	Ripley	Chautauqua	Hist. Iroquoian	W	Parker 1907 Guthe 1958:49 Yarnell 1964:124
River	N of Waterford	Saratoga	Pt. Peninsula	E	Ritchie 1958:34
Rochester Junction	Rochester Junction	Monroe	Hist. Iroquoian	C	Parker 1922:618
Rocky Rift	Little Falls	Herkimer	Prehist. Iroquoian	N	Lenig 1965:32
Rutland Hills	Black River	Jefferson	Iroquoian	N	Skinner 1921:122 Yarnell 1964:124
Sackett	Sackett	Ontario	Hist. Iroquoian	C	Hayes 1965:9
St. Lawrence	St. Lawrence	St. Lawrence	Owasco	N	Skinner 1921:155
Sand Hill 1	Fort Plain	Montgomery	Hist. Iroquoian	E	Lenig 1965:32
Scipioville, Lot 26	Scipioville	Cayuga	Hist. Iroquoian	C	Skinner 1921:52
Scotia	Scotia	Schenectady	Early Woodland	E	Ritchie 1937:186
Sea Breeze	Sea Breeze	Monroe	Pt. Peninsula	C	Ritchie 1953:3
Shelby	Shelby	Orleans	Hist. Iroquoian	W	White 1961:56
Sheridan Earthwork	Sheridan	Chautauqua	Prehist. Iroquoian	W	Guthe 1958:47
Silverheels	Brant	Erie	Prehist. Iroquoian	W	Harrington 1922:207–37 Guthe 1958:25 Yarnell 1964:124
Snell	Mohawk River	Montgomery	Owasco	E	Ritchie 1953:3 Ritchie et al. 1953:7 Guthe 1958:19
South Cruger Island	Red Hook	Dutchess	Prehist. Iroquoian	E	Ritchie 1958:81
Squawkie Hill	near Mt. Morris	Livingston	Pt. Peninsula	C	Ritchie 1937:184
Stillwater	Stillwater	Saratoga	Early Woodland	E	Ritchie 1953:3 Ritchie 1937:187 Ritchie and Dragoo 1960:Cover map
Swart-Farley	Fort Plain	Montgomery	Iroquoian	E	Lenig 1965:30
Talcott Farm	Adams	Jefferson	Iroquoian	N	Skinner notes in MAI catalogue
Theresa	Theresa	Jefferson	Iroquoian	N	Skinner 1921:146
Toll-Clute	W of Scotia	Schenectady	Early Woodland	E	Ritchie and Dragoo 1960:Fig. 1

TABLE 2 (cont.)

Site	Location*	County	Culture or Tradition	Area†	Bibliographical Data
Turnbull	Rotterdam	Schenectady	Pt. Peninsula	E	Ritchie 1953:3 Ritchie et al. 1953:27
Vine Valley	Middlesex Township	Yates	Early Woodland	C	Parker 1922:92 Ritchie 1937:186
Walsh	Fayette	Seneca	Early Woodland	C	Ritchie and Dragoo 1960:34
Watertown	Watertown	Jefferson	Hist. Iroquoian	N	Skinner 1921:162
Weaver Lake	Richfield Springs	Otsego	Prehist. Iroquoian	E	Lenig 1965:34
Westfield	Westfield	Chautauqua	Hist. Iroquoian Prehist. Iroquoian	W	Guthe 1958:25 Yarnell 1964:124
Wickham Point	Oneida Lake	Oswego	Pt. Peninsula Owasco	C	Ritchie 1953:3
Williams Mound	Genesee, Penna. (on Genesee River)	Potter Co., Penna.	Pt. Peninsula	C	Guthe 1958:18 Ritchie 1965:251
Willow Point	Willow Point	Broome	Owasco	C	Ritchie 1953:3
Willow Tree	Danube	Herkimer	Owasco	C	Ritchie et al. 1953:22
Wray	near Industry (on Genesee River)	Monroe	Pt. Peninsula	C	Ritchie 1953:3

Pipe Typology

I think it wise to introduce the following typology of pipes—the only prehistoric remains found that pertain to the smoking technology of the aborigines of this area—with an applicable note from Ritchie's introduction to his typology and nomenclature for projectile points:

> The need for some convenient classification and nomenclature to replace this awkward phraseology has grown more insistent with the progress of research. The utility of a ceramic typology for the same area encourages the effort. . . . It seems safe to predict, especially in view of the still untyped points discussed below, that continuing research within the area will lead to the addition of new types, and, with some probability, to certain revisions of the series herein mentioned. (Ritchie 1961:5)

Ritchie's key words are, of course, "addition" and "revision." An archaeological typology should be accurate, consistent, and clear, but it should also be flexible to accommodate an inevitable influx of new data. Gaps in our knowledge regarding the archaeological chronology (for example, when, how, and if the Owasco Culture diversified into the five Iroquoian cultures) complicate the task of compilation tremendously, and yet each new attempt to classify artifacts meaningfully has helped to bridge this gap. Such comprehensive typologies have been attempted by R. S. MacNeish, in his study of Iroquois pottery types (MacNeish 1952), and by Ritchie, in his typology of projectile points for New York State (Ritchie 1961).

Ideally, the sample on which a typology is based should be as large, as well documented, and as comprehensive as possible. In all cases, large or small, the researcher should state the limitations in as complete an explanation as possible. He should also state specifically his criteria.

In my research, for example, I found it most productive to proceed in the following manner. I first sorted the artifacts into two groups—stone and clay. Then, choosing morphology, both external and internal, as my main criterion, I subdivided each group into distinguishable "types"—that is, pipes complying with the given set of characteristics I had chosen, albeit at times somewhat arbitrarily. (Table 3 outlines the resulting typology.) Both stone and clay tubes are typed by internal morphology, their most distinguishing characteristic. I classified the stone pipes by general exterior shape. The clay pipes, however, were

TABLE 3

The Pipe Typology

Group	Type
	Block-end tube
	Plain-bore tube
	Platform
	Curved base
	Straight base
	Obtuse angle
Stone	Stemless bowl
	Boulder
	Vasiform
	Keel base
	Calumet
	Bar base
	Disk
	Plain-bore tube
	Discrete-chambered tube
	Simple obtuse angle
	Basket bowl
	Ring bowl
	Trumpet
Clay	Square collared
	Escutcheon
	Human effigy
	Mammal effigy
	Bird effigy
	Open-mouth effigy
	Reptile and amphibian effigy
	Miscellaneous obtuse angle

predominantly obtuse angle; therefore, I chose characteristic bowl shape and/or decoration as a differentiation factor. Into the category Miscellaneous Obtuse-Angle Pipes, I have grouped clay pipes that do not "fit" into categories as I have defined them.

Doubts arise, of course, regarding the validity of separation of archaeological artifacts into categories by the criterion of raw material. It is possible that morphology alone would yield a more logical system of grouping. However, my system presents the data so as to allow the reader to combine types of both stone and clay for his own analytic purposes (see Tables 4 and 5, in Conclusions).

That my criteria for types are arbitrary is obvious. The progression in which the types are discussed is likewise arbitrary, the general tendency being to move from the simplest in shape and decoration (for example, undecorated and incised) to the more complex (for example, effigies). The order may also indicate an archaeological chronological development, but it does not necessarily do so. It has often been difficult to decide to which category a given artifact belongs; such indecision in some cases may indicate the development of one style from another. Perhaps, then, I have presented the types in what may some day be proved to be a general time progression.

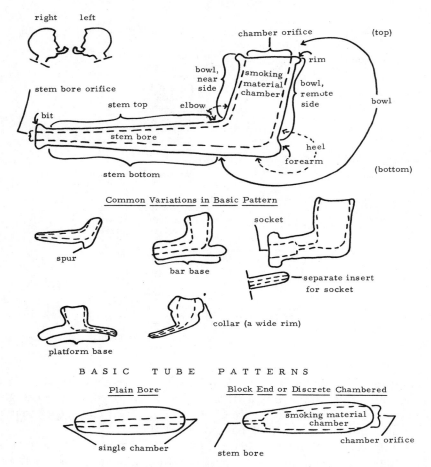

Figure 7. **Pipe and smoking tube terminology.**

To prevent confusion, I have tried to maintain consistency in my terminology. Figure 7 shows stylized pipes labeled by the terms I have chosen to describe certain specific features.

Sample Data

Following a physical description of each type is a section entitled "Discussion," in which I take up any existing pertinent data from the literature, give the statistics from my sample, and attempt, whenever possible, to interpret the type in relation to the archaeological chronology and the geographical distribution. All statistics mentioned in the discussion are summarized and evaluated in Part III, Conclusions (see Tables 4 and 5).

My sample contained 661 tubes and pipes from the Iroquois area (including artifacts from Ontario, Canada, as well as from New York State). As I explain elsewhere, and as I shall evaluate in my conclusions, a lamentable number of artifacts in private and museum collections are inadequately documented. Another factor to consider is that the museums I visited (see Acknowledgments for list) probably contain unbalanced collections of Iroquoian pipes. In using several collections, I hope that this situation has at least partially remedied itself.

Certainly a more comprehensive and better documented sample would present a more complete picture, but I believe such an undertaking to be beyond the scope of this study.

Stone Pipes

BLOCK-END TUBE
(Figs. 8–13)

Physical Characteristics

Block-end stone tubes are usually variations of a cylinder. This type includes tubes with one beveled or one flared end and bulging sides and ends. What we shall assume, for purposes of description only, to be the "smoking material" chamber is longer and larger than what we shall assume to be the stem bore (see Fig. 7).[7] The latter pierces the block end.

These tubes are usually from 2.875 to 9 inches long. The diameters of the smoking material orifice and the stem bore range from 1.25 to 1.875 inches and from 0.3125 to 1.5 inches, respectively. A wide variety of homogeneously textured stone was used in their construction. Many tubes are made of an Ohio limestone called Ohio fireclay. When

---

7. It has not been proved that these tubes were actually used for smoking; therefore, I have qualified my statements somewhat. (See discussion of the plain-bore tube.)

banded slate was used, the mineral's grain paralleled the tube's length (Douglas 1959:59).

Drilling is generally accepted as the method of construction. A blank of quarried or shaped stone was probably selected. It has been suggested that the larger smoking chamber orifice was drilled before the smaller stem-bore orifice, the latter being drilled from the block end. Finally, the tube was smoothed on its outer surfaces, a process that often yielded a high polish, especially on the finer-grained stones (Beauchamp 1897:11; Fowler 1951:14–15).

Discussion

The block-end stone tube found in the Northeastern United States, whether or not it was used as a smoking instrument, has geen generally compared in the literature with similar artifacts from Ohio of the Adena Culture. In fact, some archaeologists theorize that the Adena people dispersed from their original culture area in the Ohio Valley (see Fig. 8), possibly because of strife in their homeland following confrontation with Hopewellian peoples (Ritchie and Dragoo 1960:64). They maintain that during this dispersal, several Adena cultural traits appear in archaeological sites in the Northeast, and,

Figure 8. Provenience of block-end tubes found in the Northeast and location of the Adena heartland in Ohio. The maps and sites represented by empty circles were adapted from Douglas 1959:Fig. 3. The additional sites, indicated by filled circles, were taken from Ritchie and Dragoo 1960:Fig. 1.

accepting these traits as diagnostic of the Adena Culture's presence and/or influence, they have analyzed the extent of this dispersal (Ritchie and Dragoo 1960).

Inasmuch as there exists some doubt regarding this reconstruction of culture history for the Adena (Winters, personal communication, 1967; Griffin 1961:572), I have chosen to designate Ritchie and Dragoo's "Adena" classification for New York by "Early Woodland," thereby recognizing, but not necessarily endorsing, this dispersal theory. It is also possible that the spread of the technology involved in making such artifacts and mounds is a case of cultural borrowing, or perhaps these evidences are manifestations of the existence of a trading network. Both cultural phenomena would account for the Adena remains in the Northeast, and both seem just as likely an explanation as the dispersal theory. (See also the discussion of the stone platform pipes.)

One such Adena trait is the block-end stone tube, found in Early Woodland sites throughout the Northeast (see Fig. 8). These tubes are sometimes constructed of the aforementioned Ohio fireclay that originates from a quarry in the Adena homeland (see Fig. 8).

Three of the four block-end tubes I have examined personally were attributed to the Early Woodland Culture. One was of unknown provenience and one each was attributed to a site in the Central, Northern, and Eastern Subareas. (See Tables 4 and 5 throughout for tabulation and evaluation of data by culture and geographical area.)

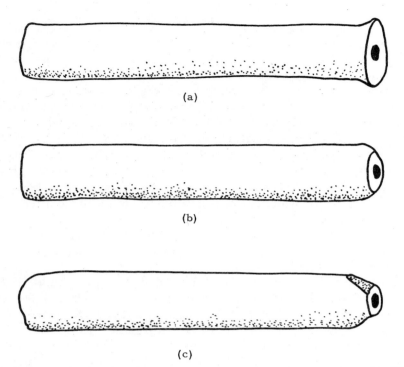

Figure 9. Three types of Adena block-end tubes, as shown in Douglas 1959: Fig. 2, 52. (a) Usual form, showing slightly flared end. (b) Straight form. (c) Beveled form. No scale appears with the figure, although Douglas comments: "Common type . . . about 9 inches long and just over an inch in diameter . . . septum or partition is, however, perforated by a relatively small hole (about ⅜″ in diameter . . .)" (Douglas 1959:53).

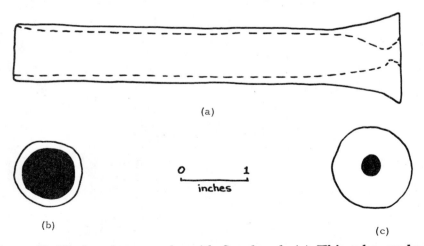

Figure 10. Block-end stone tube with flared end. (a) This tube, made of gray limestone, was found in a grave in the gravel pit at the Vine Valley site, Middlesex Township, Yates County, N. Y. Dotted lines show the inner structure. (b) Smoking chamber orifice. (c) Stem bore orifice. Rochester Museum Catalogue Number 7012. (The frequently recurring phrase "Rochester Museum Catalogue Number" will be abbreviated hereafter in the figure captions as RM.)

Scale = 1 inch.

Figure 11. Block-end stone tube with flared end. This tube, made of sandstone or steatite, was found in a grave at Palatine Bridge, Montgomery County, N. Y. (a) Left side view. (b) Smoking chamber orifice. (c) Stem bore orifice. (Beauchamp 1897:Fig. 128, 59.) Rochester Museum Collection.

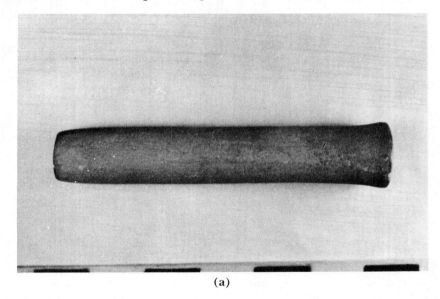

(a)

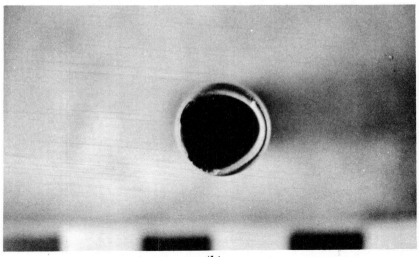

(b)

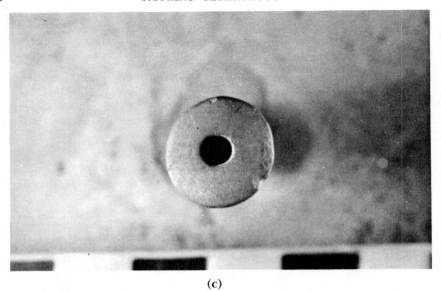

(c)

Figure 12. Block-end stone tube of green slate banded with tan, found in Woodland mound on Long Sault Island in the Saint Lawrence River near Massena, N. Y. (a) Side view. (b) Stem bore orifice. (c) Smoking chamber orifice. Heye Foundation Museum of the American Indian Catalogue Number 8/6227. (The frequently recurring phrase "Heye Foundation Museum of the American Indian Catalogue Number" will be abbreviated hereafter in the figure captions as HFMAI.)

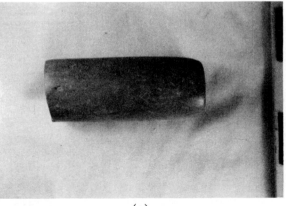

(a)

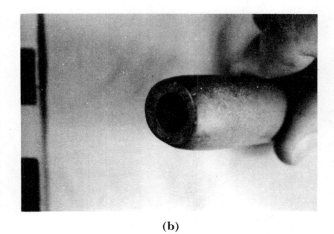

(b)

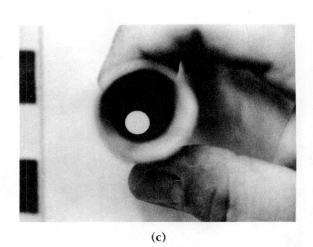

(c)

Figure 13. Cigar-shaped, block-end stone tube of reddish brown sandstone from Bridgehampton, Long Island, N. Y. (a) Side view. (b) Stem bore orifice. (c) Smoking chamber orifice. William Wallace Tooker Collection, HFMAI 23/1670.

(a)

(b)

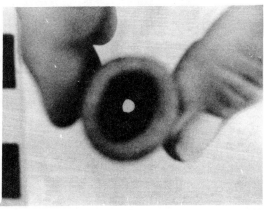

(c)

PLAIN-BORE TUBE
(Figs. 14-21)

Physical Characteristics

Tubes of this type have several exterior shapes: slightly oval, bulging toward one end, and straight. All examples are considerably longer than they are wide and have in common a chamber or inner surface that is relatively homogeneous in diameter, a feature distinguishing them from the block-end tubes.

The construction material of these tubes varies. The most common are grained sedimentary slate and limestone, raw materials often used by the prehistoric inhabitants in the manufacture of other items, such as birdstones, gorgets, and banner stones.

We can only guess at the construction methods, but the inside bore was apparently drilled by a friction method; I shall discuss this procedure in detail when I take up the construction of platform pipes. The outside of the tube was usually smoothed to an even finish.

Discussion

I have personally examined only seven of these tubes; therefore, I have also used illustrations and examples of this type of artifact as it has been recorded by other researchers. The importance of this early smoking tube justifies the combination of my scanty data with that from collections I have studied but not seen so that meaningful correlations can be drawn.

The geographical distribution of the plain-bore stone tube is wide; however, most findings have been made in the Central Subarea: four in the Central Subarea; one each in the Western, Eastern, and Southern Subareas. Although my study is primarily concerned with this subarea and my sampling is too small to be considered truly random, I believe we can assume that the data reflect, to some degree, the approximate distribution of this type.

Of the seven tubes I actually studied, only one was attributable to an identifiable site—Early Woodland. The literature corroborates this dating: Ritchie writes that the "smoking pipes of tubular varieties —the cigar-shaped and the specialized block-end type—are Early Woodland innovations" (Ritchie 1965:178).

That these artifacts were used as pipes has been doubted by several researchers, who argue that they lack too many pipe features (Morgan 1952:87). Doubt accompanied by an open mind regarding function is, in my opinion, an attribute, but in this instance I believe we have sufficient evidence from other cultures where similar artifacts have been found and proved to have been used in smoking that our inclusion of these tubes as smoking instruments is most probably correct.

The Mayan bas reliefs illustrated by Dunhill (Dunhill 1924:23–24, 30) show several men smoking such tubes (see Fig. 14). It is an interesting speculation that similar artifacts were used in the North American woodlands and in Meso America, the home and possibly the source of tobacco (Gleason 1952:204).

I must point out that the Mayan examples illustrated are all from the Classic period in Mexico and date from long after their counterparts in the eastern woodlands and American Southwest; the documentation for use of these tubes as pipes between 1500 and 1000 B.C., or earlier, in eastern North America, is well documented (Winters, personal communication, 1967).

Figure 14. Mayan bas reliefs showing men smoking tubes similar to the plain-bore tubes of the North American aborigine. (a) Mayan man in reclining position smoking a tube (Dunhill 1924:30). (b) Mayan priest smoking a tube—part of a bas relief on the Temple of the Cross at Palenque, Chiapas, Mexico (Dunhill 1924:23). (c) Mayan man smoking a tubular pipe (Dunhill 1924:24). No scale.

(a)

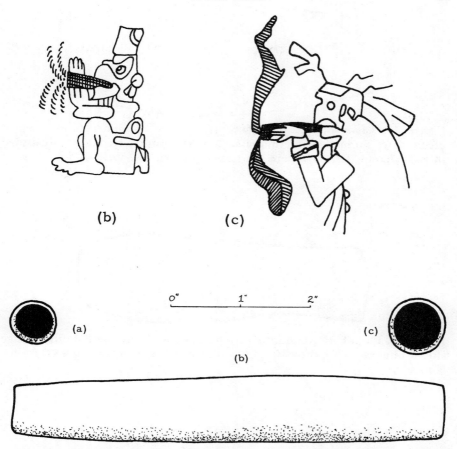

Figure 15. Plain-bore stone tube of undecorated, fine-grained, gray lime-stone mottled with brown. (a) Stem bore orifice. (b) View of left side. (c) Smoking chamber orifice. From the South Bay site, Washington County, N. Y. HFMAI 22/280.

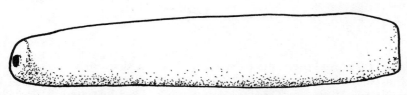

Figure 16. Undecorated plain-bore tube of black-banded gray slate. From the Camillus site, Onondaga County, N. Y. (As illustrated in Beauchamp 1897:53, where the scale is given as 5.4 inches long and with a chamber width of 1 inch.)

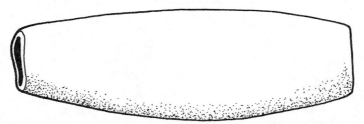

Figure 17. Cigar-shaped, plain-bore stone tube of undecorated, striped green slate. From the Palermo site, Oswego County, N. Y. (As illustrated in Beauchamp 1897:53, where the length is given as 7 inches.)

Figure 18. Plain-bore stone tube with bulbar end. From the Palatine Bridge site, Montgomery County, N. Y. (As illustrated in Beauchamp 1897:53–54. No scale.)

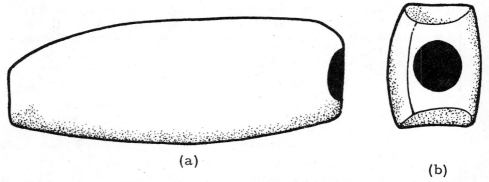

(a)

(b)

Figure 19. Plain-bore stone tube, cigar shape evident, of undecorated, dark green, striped slate. (a) Right side. (b) Smoking chamber orifice. From the Oswego River site, Oswego County, N. Y. (As illustrated in Beauchamp 1897:53, where the scale is given as follows: length, 3.5 inches; chamber width—large end, shown here—0.5625 inch; chamber width—small end— 0.385 inch.)

Figure 20. Plain-bore stone tube with constricted area and tapered end. Undecorated gray slate with light brown banding. (a) Angled view showing top. (b) Side view. From the Tuscarora Reservation, Niagara County, N. Y. W. Mackay Collection, HFMAI 8/8405. Scale on photographs.

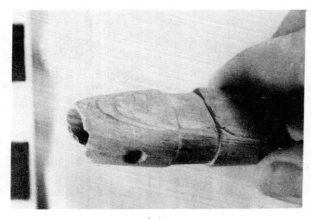

(a)

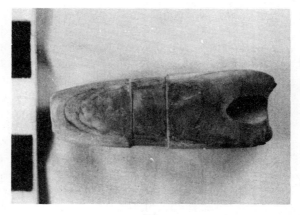

(b)

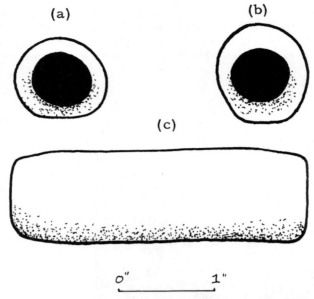

Figure 21. **Plain-bore stone tube with slightly flattened side, of undeco-rated gray slate with black banding. (a) Smoking chamber orifice. (b) Stem bore orifice. (c) View of left side. From the Peekskill site, Westchester County, N. Y. G. W. Sykes Collection, HFMAI 12/648.**

PLATFORM
(Figs. 22–31)

Physical Characteristics

I. *Curved-base platform pipe.* This type of platform pipe shows a curve in its bottom surface when it is viewed from the side. A cross section would reveal variations in shape from almost oval to a flattened form with lateral ridges. Near the center of this platform and at its highest point is the bowl, which extends vertically and varies in shape from vasiform to tapering. The bowls are circular or slightly oval when viewed from above.

II. *Straight-base platform pipe.* This type is very similar to the curved-base platform except that its base is straight and not curved. It is important as a variation for reasons I shall discuss later.

The interior features of the platform pipes include a large drilled or gouged chamber within the bowl. A connecting stem bore extends from one end of the platform to the bowl. Most specimens are made of Ohio pipestone or fireclay, imported into the area (see Fig. 8), and steatite, which was often finished with a high polish.

In discussing the method of construction, I shall digress from hypothesis to summarize what various students have discovered about what they assume to have been the aboriginal lithic industry. Beauchamp has stated that the artifacts to be drilled were first blocked out and drilled in a rough form; their outer contours were smoothed after the drilling was completed (Beauchamp 1897:11).

In his account of his own experiments with aboriginal methods of stoneworking at the Oaklawn steatite quarry in Cranston, Rhode Island, Fowler made a steatite pipe with a drilled stem bore in the following manner. He first pecked the stone from the quarry matrix. Pecking seems to have been the preferable method because stones have been found with pipe outlines pecked into them before they were discarded (Fig. 22a). He then reamed out the bowl with a quartzite reamer, many of which were found at the site. Fowler used two reamers of different size for this process: the larger was used to form the bowl chamber; the smaller gave the tapered effect to the bottom of the bowl chamber (Fig. 22b).

Fowler assumed that the next step in the process was the drilling of the stem bore. Because no stone drills of a small size were found at the quarry site, he hypothesized that the drilling was accomplished with a more destructible material. Although he noted that bone or antler might have been used, he chose to work with wooden drills and a fine abrasive sand. By this method, he could drill a stem bore 0.25 inch in diameter at the bit end and 0.0625 inch in diameter at the juncture with the bowl chamber. During this task, he averaged 0.0625 to 0.1875 inch per hour.

Finally, he removed the rough edges from the outside of the bowl and smoothed the outer surface. The total time required by the process, except for the stem bore drilling, was 7 hours; from his rate, I estimate that the stem bore took him about 20 hours. The job represents, then, up to four days labor for the aborigine working in the quarry during daylight hours.

It is interesting that the aborigine devoted this much time to the manufacture of what we consider a nonessential item. However, the pipemaker may have obtained his material at the quarry in just a few hours and returned home to work at his leisure. Our time estimate is probably incorrect, furthermore, inasmuch as we cannot expect Fowler, an uninstructed neophyte, to excel in his first attempt at what appears to have been a skilled art (Fowler 1951:13).

Discussion

I must refer to the literature for discussion of the archaeological chronology, for of the 15 artifacts of this type that I studied, none was dated by museum records or by the literature. The two curved-base

platform pipes I examined were from the Northern and Eastern Subareas. Of the 13 straight-base platform pipes I studied, 5 were attributed to the Central Subarea, 1 each to the Western, Northern,
Eastern, and Southern Subareas, and 3 to the Neutral Area of Ontario,
Canada. The 5 found in the Central Subarea may reflect the popu-
larity of the sites in this area within the collections I have studied.
One straight-base platform pipe was of unknown provenience, other
than New York State.

Ritchie maintains, as I have already discussed in my introduction to
Part II, that platform pipes, often known as "mound-builders' pipes,"
seem to have been imported by the Hopewellian people and later
copied locally. He continues by pointing out that the Squawkie Hill
sites near Mount Morris, Livingston County, ". . . included burials
in stone cist graves, accompanied by such unequivocally Hopewellian
artifacts as curved-base platform pipes of Ohio fireclay. . . ." (Ritchie
1965:214; see Figs. 24 and 25). He asserts that the Squawkie Hill
people migrated to the Iroquois area from the south.

However, I must point out that unfortunately no habitation sites
have as yet been recognized in New York State. Furthermore, although
Ritchie presents the curved-base platform pipe as appearing in the
nuclear-mound culture and states that the straight-base platform pipe
is a modification of the curved-base variety (Ritchie 1965:225), no one
else makes this speculation. Morgan simply states that in Ohio both
types are found concurrently (Morgan 1952:90). Both Ritchie and
Morgan mention crude animal effigies appearing on these pipes. I
found no such examples.

Most students believe that these pipes were of religious significance
to the Hopewellian people. They were included in the grave goods
of the mortuary mounds characteristic of these people, and, after their
usefulness as smoking instruments had passed, they were kept, almost,
as Ritchie says, "to have been cherished as heirlooms" (Ritchie
1965:232). I have found that the edges of the broken pipes were
worn smooth—that is, possibly reworked so that they could be reused.
For example, one pipe was drilled in eight places so that the broken
pieces could be laced together (White site, Chenango County—a
Hunter's Home site of the Late Point Peninsula Culture; Ritchie
1965:256; see Fig. 31).

Further studies should be made of the central Ohio Hopewellian
area to determine what correlations, if any, can be made between
the Ohio and New York artifact assemblages of platform pipes.

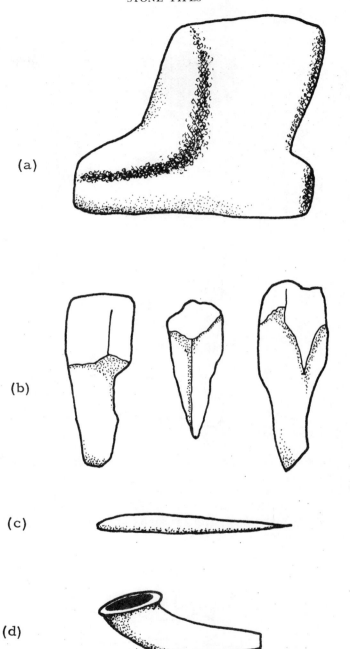

Figure 22. (a) A piece of stone found in quarry rubble in which a pipe blank has been pecked. (b) Three quartzite reamers found in quarry rubble. Fowler used similar ones in his own pipemaking. (c) Wooden drill of the type used by Fowler to work the stem bore of pipes. (d) Finished stone pipe made by Fowler (Fowler 1951:13; no scale given for a–d).

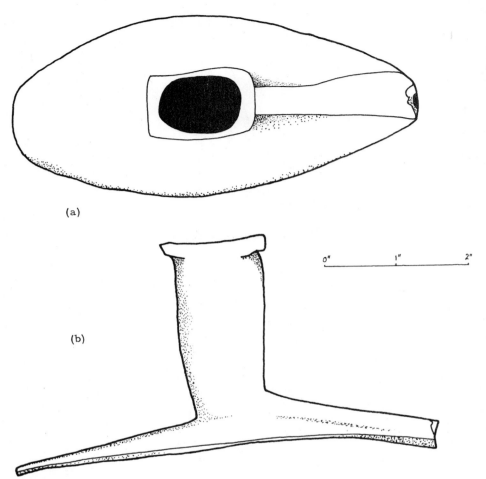

(a)

(b)

Figure 23. Curved-base platform pipe with leaf-shaped base. Constructed of green and black mottled steatite. The rim of the bowl is distinct but damaged. (a) View from the top into the smoking material chamber. (b) View from the left side. From the Kinderhook site, Columbia County, N. Y. E. van Alstyne Collection, HFMAI 18/1605.

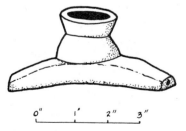

Figure 24. Curved-base platform pipe of gray, tan, and red fireclay. From the Squawkie Hill site, Mound I, Livingston County, N. Y. (As illustrated in Ritchie 1938:9; 1944:203. Scale is on drawing.)

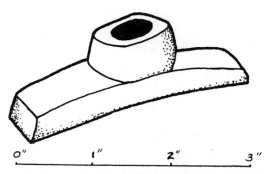

Figure 25. Curved-base platform pipe of dusty pink pipestone or fireclay. The bowl was apparently broken and smoothed off later. (As illustrated in Ritchie 1938:13; 1944:205. Scale is on drawing.)

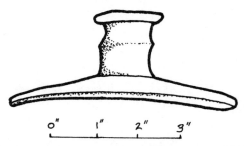

Figure 26. Curved-base platform pipe of dark steatite with incised orna-mentation. From the Jack's Reef site, Onondaga County, N. Y. K. O. Palmer Collection, Syracuse, N. Y. (As illustrated in Ritchie 1944:149. Scale is on drawing.)

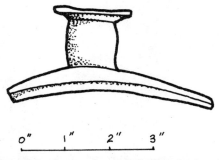

Figure 27. Curved-base platform pipe of dark steatite. From Point Penin-sula site, Jefferson County, N. Y. Collection of J. B. Nichols, Cape Vincent, N. Y. (As illustrated in Ritchie 1944:165. Scale is on drawing.)

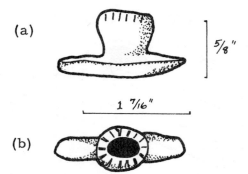

(a)

5/8"

1 7/16"

(b)

Figure 28. Miniature straight-base platform pipe, stem bore undrilled. Steatite. (a) Side view. (b) View into the smoking material chamber. From the Squawkie Hill site, Livingston County, N. Y. (As illustrated in Ritchie 1938:32. Scale is on drawing.)

Figure 29. Straight-base platform pipe, undecorated, of fine-grained, hard, green stone. (a) View from the top into the smoking material chamber. (b) View of the right side. (c) Photograph of right side. From South Bay site, Washington County, N. Y. E. Burke Collection, HFMAI 22/279.

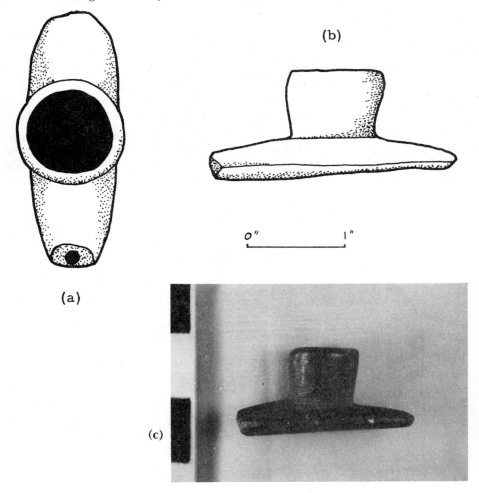

(b)

0"   1"

(a)

(c)

Figure 30. Straight-base platform pipe in a very worn condition. Undecorated reddish brown steatite. (a) View from the side. (b) View from the top into the smoking material chamber. (c) Angled view showing depth. (d) View into smoking material chamber. Seneca County. W. C. Wyman Collection, HFMAI 18/5481.

(a)

(b)

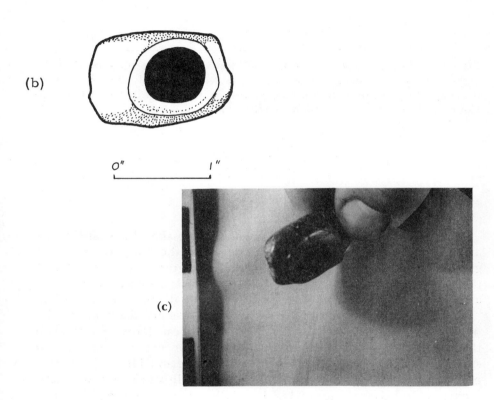

(c)

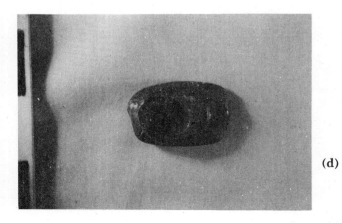

(d)

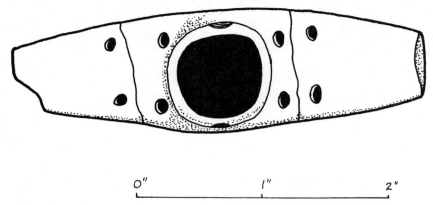

Figure 31. Straight-base platform pipe viewed from the top, showing the eight holes drilled near the breaks. Laces were probably drawn through these apertures to bind the broken pieces. From the White site, Chenango County, N. Y. (As illustrated in Ritchie 1965:256.)

OBTUSE ANGLE
(Figs. 32–42)

Physical Characteristics

The obtuse-angle pipe is so named because the elbow angle, the angle formed by the junction of the stem and the bowl, is obtuse, or greater than 90 degrees and less than 180 degrees. Cross sections of the stem reveal round or ridged sides; the bowls are usually rounded, although some show slight ridges at the side and distinct rim definition.

Pipes of this variety that I have seen are usually made of steatite or limestone and show no evidence that European tools were used in their construction. The chamber is gouged or drilled and finished smoothly, the stem bore drilled with great accuracy. The outer surface may have a smooth to a polished finish. In the illustrations that follow, I have included drawings of blanks to illustrate a stage in this pipe's manufacture.

Discussion

I studied 13 obtuse-angle stone pipes in my research. Of these, 6 were from the Neutral Area of Ontario, Canada, and 7 were from

New York State—3 each from the Northern and Central Subareas and 1 from the Western Subarea. Only two of these seven were identifiable: one was dated to the Owasco Culture and the other to the Iroquoian.

I can make few conclusions about this type of pipe other than the preceding description of its geographical distribution. In some instances, it seems to show platform pipe features, such as lateral ridges on the stem; in other examples, it seems to parallel the style of the obtuse-angle pipes of clay, which I shall discuss in the next section. The latter variety may, in fact, owe its resemblance to its clay counterpart, which was first found in Kipp Island sites of the Late Point Peninsula and Owasco Cultures, when these stone examples were made (Ritchie 1965:228).

Literature on the stone obtuse-angle pipe is scarce because of its rarity. Slightly bent stone examples occur early in the Kipp Island Phase of the Late Point Peninsula Culture (Ritchie 1965:228). These obtuse-angle pipes and their clay likenesses increase in number during the Late Hunter's Home Phase of the same culture (Ritchie 1965:254).

Finally, in the Owasco Culture, the ratio of stone obtuse-angle pipes to pottery obtuse-angle pipes in the same sites becomes very uneven, with the latter prevalent. These stone pipes are reportedly made of steatite or chlorite schist and are usually undecorated (Ritchie 1965:294).

Figure 32. Stone obtuse-angle pipe of black steatite with one ridge extending along each side of the stem. (a) Drawing of right side. (b) Photograph of right side. From the Smithville site, Jefferson County, N. Y. A. A. Getman Collection, HFMAI /9886.

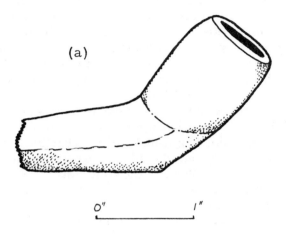

(a)

0" _____ 1"

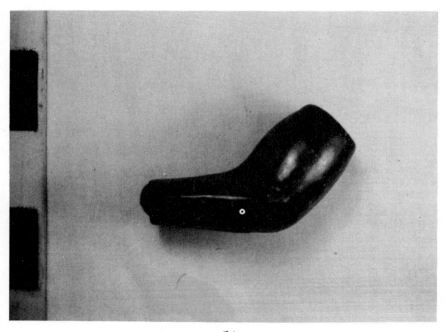

(b)

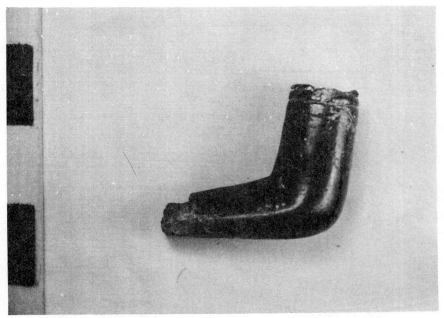

Figure 33. Stone obtuse-angle pipe of black steatite with one ridge extending along each side of the stem and incised lines forming the rim. From
the St. Lawrence site, Jefferson County, N. Y. A. A. Getman Collection,
HFMAI /9885.

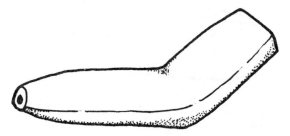

Figure 34. Stone obtuse-angle pipe of black soapstone. **Lateral ridges as in
Figs. 32 and 33, but extending along the sides of the bowl as well as the
stem.** From the Seneca Falls site, Genesee County, N. Y. (As illustrated in
Beauchamp 1897:50, where the pipe is described as 2.75 inches long.)

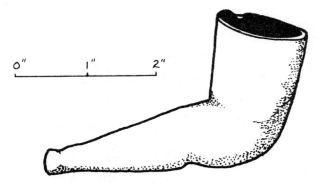

Figure 35. Stone obtuse-angle pipe of steatite. From grave of Vine Valley site, Yates County, N. Y. (As illustrated in Ritchie 1944:191. Scale on drawing.)

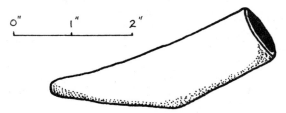

Figure 36. Plain stone obtuse-angle pipe of Onondaga chert. From Geneseo Mound site (Big Tree Farm site in Table 2), Livingston County, N. Y. (As illustrated in Ritchie 1944:226. Scale is on drawing.)

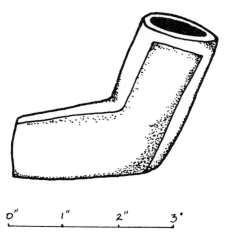

Figure 37. Stone obtuse-angle pipe of limestone with a squared bowl formed by raised ridges at the four corners. From Caine Mound site, Erie County, N. Y. A. C. Glamm, Jr. Collection. (As illustrated in Ritchie 1965:219. Scale is on drawing.)

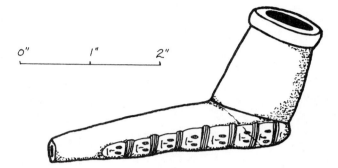

Figure 38. Stone obtuse-angle pipe of steatite showing a row of human effigies on the side of the stem. From Bettysburg site, Chenango County, N. Y. (As illustrated in Ritchie 1965:294. Scale is on drawing.)

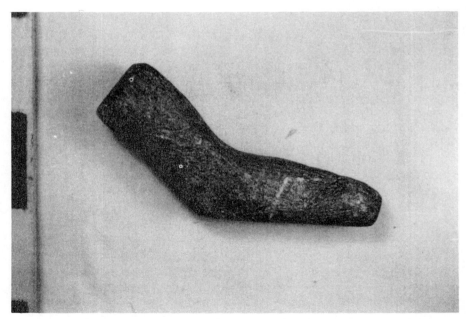

Figure 39. Obtuse-angle pipe blank of steatite. Rudimentary beginnings of drilling appear on the stem bore and the chamber of the bowl. From the Black River site, Jefferson County, N. Y. A. Skinner Collection, HFMAI 9/3252.

Figure 40. (a) Stone obtuse-angle pipe blank of gray limestone. Rudimentary drilling appears on the smoking material chamber and the stem bore (b). From the Phelp's Farm site, Jefferson County, N. Y. RM 19482.

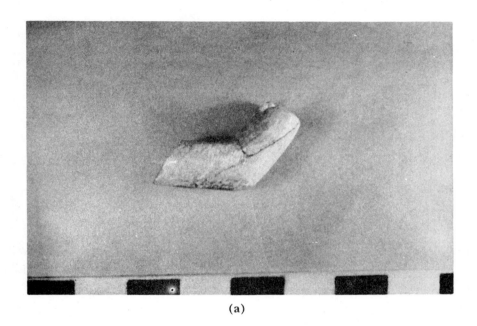

(a)

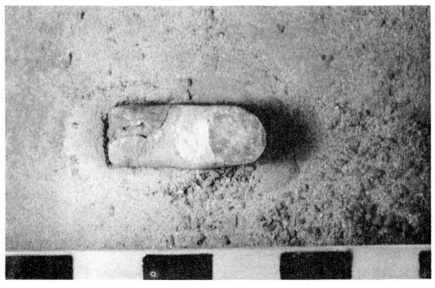

(b)

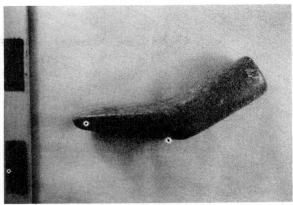

Figure 41. View of right side of gray stone obtuse-angle pipe with a ridge along each side of stem. From Lake Medad, Ontario, Canada. L. J. Mullock and J. O. McGregor Collection, HFMAI 5/7137.

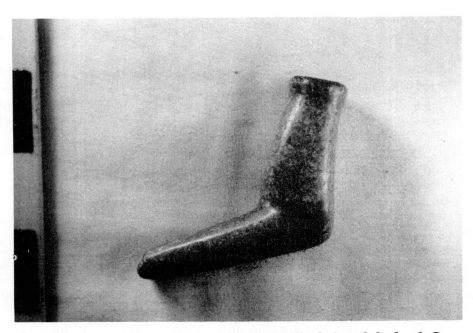

Figure 42. Stone obtuse-angle pipe with basketlike bulge of the bowl. Gray stone; perforated base is not shown. From Grand River (near Middleport), Ontario, Canada. W. J. Bryant Collection, HFMAI 10/3675.

STEMLESS BOWL: BOULDER, VASIFORM, AND KEEL BASE

The three types that I shall now discuss may be classified as one group—stemless-bowl pipes: boulder-bowl pipes, the crudest of the three; vasiform pipes, the intermediate form; keel-base pipes, showing the most work. All are pipe bowls that were apparently used with wooden stems; several stem materials might have been used, but we may at least hypothesize that wood was one, for ethnographic collections of pipes from Indians of the Northeastern woodlands contain keel-base pipes having wooden stems. Many of the bowls have been perforated in their bases, probably for the insertion of a decorative and protective fob, which I shall discuss in detail following the illustrations for the keel-base pipe (see also Figs. 67 and 68).

Most pipes of this general classification have been dated to the Iroquoian Culture. Data from the collections and the literature are insufficient for more precise dating, and, although further study of stemless-bowl pipes of the Iroquois area may prove the present information incorrect, we shall accept it for study purposes now.

BOULDER BOWL
(Figs. 43–48)

Physical Characteristics

I have described a boulder-bowl pipe as any stone or boulder that has been drilled to form a pipe bowl and the exterior surface of which has not been extensively shaped, altered, or smoothed. Specimens are usually of the workable sedimentary stone but exceptions are numerous, and we can say that examples can be made from almost any locally available material.

This type was manufactured by gouging and drilling from two directions—from the stem socket and from the smoking material chamber orifice. The latter is larger than the former, which was made to receive a stem of some perishable material, probably wood.

Discussion

Of the six boulder-bowl pipes I studied, only two could be dated; both were attributed to the Iroquoian Culture. Three pipes were found in the Western Subarea, two in the Central Subarea, and one in Huronia, Ontario, Canada.

This relatively small sampling has led me to doubt the validity of establishing this pipe as a representative type; therefore, I do so with qualifications. I expect that continued study will enable archaeologists to date more accurately this pipe's place in the chronology. It may also establish that this boulder variety is an incipient vasiform style, or perhaps merely the unfinished vasiform pipe itself, although several examples I studied seem to have been stained by use.

No pipes of this description were discussed or illustrated in the literature. They may have been grouped with the vasiform pipes. It is also possible that the type is unique to the collections I have seen.

Figure 43. Boulder-bowl pipe of sandstone from the Cattaraugus Reservation, Cattaraugus County, N. Y. W. J. Bryant Collection, HFMAI 10/3671. (a) View into smoking material chamber orifice. (b) View into stem socket on near side of bowl.

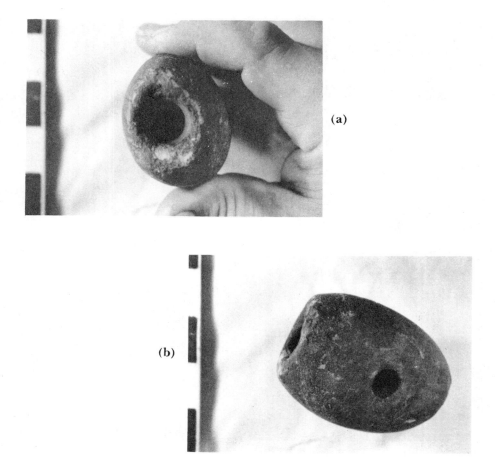

(a)

(b)

Figure 44. Boulder-bowl pipe of light brown sedimentary stone, possibly limestone. (a) View of right side showing slight shaping of outer surface and incised line ringing the upper bowl. (b) View into chamber orifice. Schoharie County. RM 20327.

(a)

(b)

Figure 45. Boulder-bowl pipe of brown sedimentary stone with slightly shaped outer surface. The distinct rim area is slightly damaged, and two sets of incised lines appear on the left side of the bowl. From Chenango Lake, Broome County, N. Y. A. Mather Collection, HFMAI 16/1761.

Figure 46. Boulder-bowl pipe with slightly modified outer surface. Note stem socket on near side of bowl. The rim area shows incised "X"'s and the base of the bowl is perforated. From a Neutral village, Kienuka, Niagara County. W. Mackay Collection. HFMAI 8/8537.

Figure 47. (a) Side view of boulder-bowl pipe with modified exterior surface.
Gray steatite. There are three horizontal grooves in the bowl, each of
which is decorated with incising or notches. (b) View into chamber orifice.
From Old Fort, Cayuga County, N. Y. RM 584.

(a)

(b)

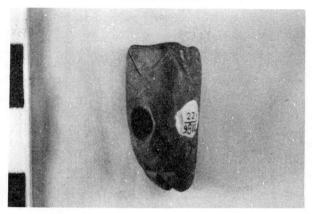

Figure 48. Boulder-bowl pipe with modified exterior of brown sedimentary stone. Side view shows the stem socket on near side of bowl. The base is notched in a cross pattern that resembles a deer's hoof. This "notch" could also represent a broken base perforation. The rim is incised in a "V" design. From a grave in Perry City, Tompkins County, N. Y. Collected by G. Fisher in 1846. HFMAI 22/9812.

VASIFORM
(Figs. 49–58)

Physical Characteristics

These pipes are approximately the same size as the boulder-bowl pipes, but their exteriors have been shaped and smoothed until they have achieved a vaselike or cone-shaped appearance. The bowl rim is sometimes distinct, even flared, and the bowl is often incised. Some examples are perforated near the base. A fob attached at this point probably connected the bowl to the stem. The vasiform pipe was most often constructed of sedimentary stone, with steatite, limestone, sandstone, and even quartzite being used.

The stem socket and the smoking material chamber were probably gouged and drilled concurrently, the smaller aperture becoming the stem socket and the larger, the chamber. The fob aperture was drilled below the chamber in the base. The outer surface varies from barely smooth to polished.

Discussion

Six vasiform pipes were identifiable: one was dated to the Owasco Culture and five were attributed to the Iroquoian. The data thus place this pipe in the Late Woodland Stage. Of a total of 37 vasiform pipes studied, 20 were from sites in Ontario, Canada. Thirteen were concentrated in the Central Subarea, and the remaining four pipes were scattered, one each in the Western and Northern Subareas and two in the Eastern Subarea.

The literature generally substantiates the geographical distribution indicated by these tabulations. In reading commentary concerning western New York archaeology, I discovered that vasiform pipes were found all around the Great Lakes and eastward into Pennsylvania and New York. They are found in late prehistoric to early historic sites (Witthoft *et al.* 1953:94).

In a discussion of the pipes from the Adams and Tram sites in Livingston County, Wray and Schoff (1953:54) report that they found only a few stone pipes of the vasiform style and only one other pipe—a crude clay example. Apparently, then, smoking was not extremely popular among the Indians of these late prehistoric Iroquoian sites in New York (1550–57), and the stone-bowl pipe was the major smoking instrument. Shell inlays and pipe dottle in Seneca burials of this period, however, may indicate that wooden pipes, since rotted, were used (Wray and Schoff 1953:54).

In another Seneca site of the late prehistoric period, Dutch Hollow in Livingston County, vasiform pipes were found. They were thought to have been imports from the Erie and Neutral sources—tribes to the west along the Great Lakes (Ritchie 1954:95).

In conclusion, I feel that a diffusional study of vasiform pipes in sites west of the Iroquois area might establish whether this type indeed actually did pass from west to east and at what time this diffusion might have occurred. Such an investigation might also help to solve the riddle of why the number of pipes found in Seneca sites dwindles from an early large number of many varieties to a few vasiforms in sites dated as late as the last half of the sixteenth century (Wray 1956A:15).

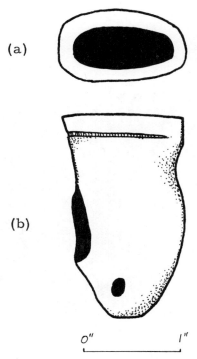

(a)

(b)

0"   1"

Figure 49. Vasiform pipe of black steatite with perforated base. (a) View into chamber orifice. (b) View of right side showing perforation. From Bristol Center (West Side), Ontario County, N. Y. HFMAI 2/6446.

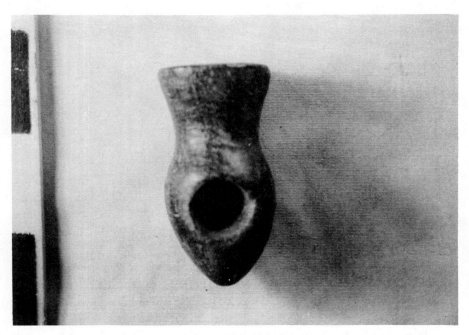

Figure 50. Vasiform pipe of hard greenish black stone, with a perforated base. View shows near side of bowl, with stem socket and base perforation. From Gus Warren site, Ontario County, N. Y. H. L. Schoff Collection, HFMAI 22/3528.

Figure 51. Vasiform pipe (damaged) of gray stone with a perforated base (base perforation not visible here). From Niagara County, N. Y. W. Mackay Collection, HFMAI 8/8406.

(a)   (b)

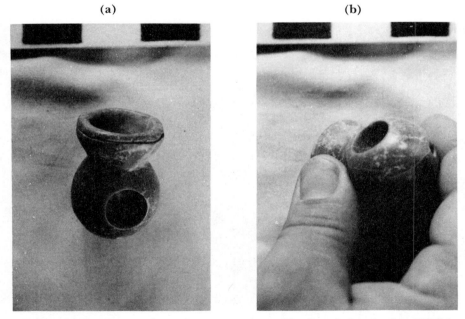

Figure 52. Vasiform pipe of tan steatite with flared bowl rim. Highly polished and having a perforated base. (a) View of stem socket in near side of bowl. (b) Base perforation view. From Neutral village, Kienuka site, Niagara County, N. Y. W. Mackay Collection, HFMAI 8/8536.

Figure 53. Vasiform pipe of tan steatite with perforated base and incised hourglass figures on the sides. (a) Side view showing base perforation. (b) Near side of bowl, showing stem socket. (c) Smoking chamber orifice. From Dutch Hollow site, Livingston County, N. Y. RM AR 27779.

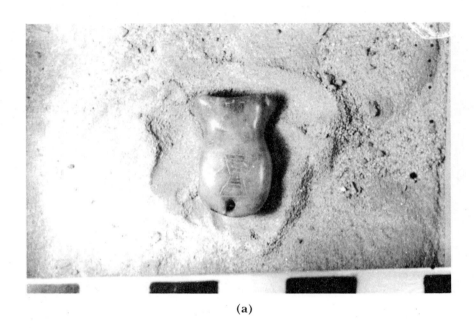

(a)

(b)

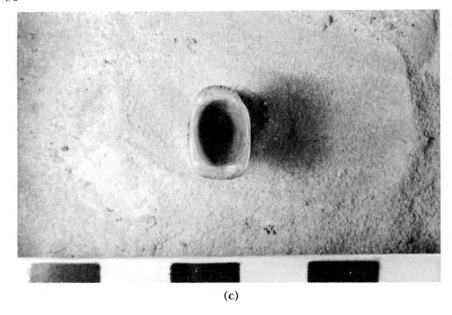

(c)

Figure 54. Vasiform pipe of gray, polished steatite. View is of left side of bowl, showing base perforation. From Ontario, Canada. HFMAI 20/6455.

Figure 55. Vasiform pipe with cone-shaped base, constructed of white quartzite. (a) View of near side of bowl, showing stem socket. (b) View into chamber orifice. From Rome, Oneida County, N. Y. RM 20330.

(a)

(b)

Figure 56. Vasiform pipe of tan sandstone with cone-shaped base. View is of near side of bowl, showing stem socket. From Cayuga County, N. Y. HFMAI 20/6425.

Figure 57. Vasiform pipe of gray steatite with a cone-shaped base. (a) View of near side of bowl, showing stem socket. Bowl is decorated with incised lines and punctate marks. (b) View into chamber orifice. From Onondaga County, N. Y. RM 20326.

(a)

(b)

Figure 58. Vasiform pipe with a keel base of black steatite. This pipe could easily be transitional between vasiform and keel types, for it appears to have characteristics of both. View of right side shows base perforation and stem socket. From Old Castle, Ontario County, N. Y. RM 9080.

KEEL BASE
(Figs. 59–66)

Physical Characteristics

Keel-base pipes are so named for their shape; beneath the vasiform bowl is a constricted area that widens again into a base resembling a boat's keel. This keel section includes the stem socket and the base of the chamber. It is oblong or rectangular, flaring below the con- striction and tapering again toward its bottom. A spur often protrudes below the keel. Decorations may vary, among them distinctive rim markers, incising on the keel, and a unique shape or design to the keel base, such as a row of scallops. A fob perforation is usually evident in the bottom of the keel, or in the spur, if present.

The keel-base pipe is made most often of local sedimentary rock; limestone and steatite are among the most common materials. When imported stones are used, Ohio firestone and Minnesota catlinite are common. This style of pipe has been copied in pottery, but such examples are rare and thus considered atypical. One keel-base pipe from Livingston County is constructed of antler.

These pipes are fine examples of aboriginal stonework. Many show signs of having been worked with European metal tools.

Discussion

I studied five keel-base pipes from identifiable sites, all of which are dated to the Iroquoian Culture. Thirteen New York examples are identifiable geographically: 12 from the Central Subarea and 1 from the Northern Subarea. Of the 10 Canadian examples, 8 were from sites in the Neutral Area of Ontario and 1 each was from the Huronia and St. Lawrence River Areas. From these data we can hypothesize that this type of pipe was of the Iroquoian Culture and that it was probably more prevalent in the Central Subarea of New York and in Ontario, Canada, than in the other subareas. Its scarcity in the Western Subarea is puzzling and warrants further investigation after more data have been uncovered.

This particular style of pipe is mentioned in the literature very often, where it is referred to as the "micmac" pipe, after the Lab- radorian tribe (Driver 1964:Map 40). This terminology is unfor- tunate, for although ethnographers have found this pipe in use among these northern peoples, its archaeological spread encompasses the entire Great Lakes region, and it may be that the pipe was developed to be used in the calumet ritual during its spread into the Iroquois area.

In checking further into the geographical distribution of this type, I discovered that tribes of the northern pine forests have made and used keel-base pipes recently. Naskapi, Montagnais, and Abnaki ethnographic collections in the Heye Foundation Museum of the American Indian and in the Smithsonian Institution contain recent examples of this pipe. William Stiles, a curator at the Museum of the American Indian and a visitor among the Montagnais, has told me that when these Indians are unable to trade for manufactured pipes, they make stone keel-base bowl pipes to be smoked with hollow wooden stems (Stiles, personal communication, 1966).

Much has been written about this type of pipe in the historical period. From the contact period to 1700, pipes were made in clay in increasing numbers. After 1700, however, there occurred a revival of stone pipemaking, and the prevalent type made was the keel-base bowl pipe (Wray 1956A:16).

Several archaeologists feel that the shape of the keel-base pipe is a modification of the calumet pipe of the northern plains and the vasiform bowl pipe of the Great Lakes. They believe that it never became a popular style in the Five Nations villages but spread rapidly into Ontario and the northern tribes (Witthoft et al. 1953:95). Comparison of the keel-base bowl pipe with certain calumet styles reveals that both have a bar base (keel), both show a perforation, both have similar decorations (effigies, etc.), and, finally, stem decorations of Naskapi and plains types are similar (Witthoft et al. 1953:90).

I find no reason for not concurring with the opinion of these archaeologists for the present. Therefore, the keel pipes were probably ". . . diffuse copies of plains calumets, used in a somewhat parallel and historically related tobacco ritual" (Witthoft et al. 1953:90).

Figure 59. Keel-base bowl pipe of gray steatite. (a) Side view. (b) **Near side of bowl, showing stem socket. (c) Pipe bottom, showing perforation. From Monroe County, N. Y. H. L. Schoff Collection, HFMAI 22/2955.**

(a)

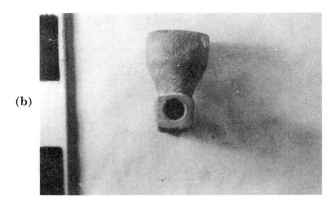

(b)

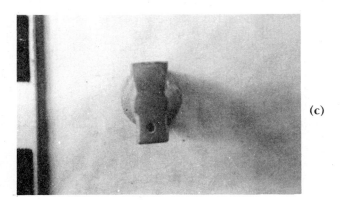

(c)

Figure 60. Keel-base bowl pipe, with incised, double semicircles appearing on all sides of the bowl except the near side (b), which shows one semicircle. (a) Chamber orifice. (c) View of left side, showing base perforation. From site on the west side of Canandaigua Lake, Ontario County, N. Y. RM 2090.

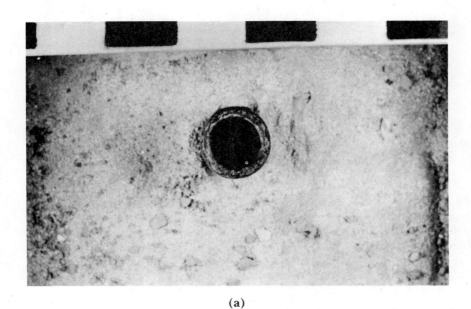

(a)

(b)

(c)

Figure 61. Keel-base bowl pipe of brown stone. (a) View of near side of bowl, showing stem socket. View (b) shows the incised "X" pattern within a box design on the sides of the keel. From the Onondaga Reservation, Onondaga County, N. Y. J. Keppler Collection, HFMAI 14/5689.

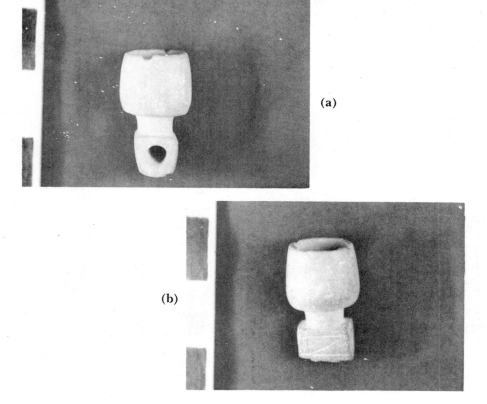

(a)

(b)

Figure 62. Keel-base bowl pipe of tan steatite. (a) View of left side showing curved, perforated keel. (b) View of near side of bowl, showing stem socket. From Seneca Lake, Ontario County, N. Y. RM 10130.

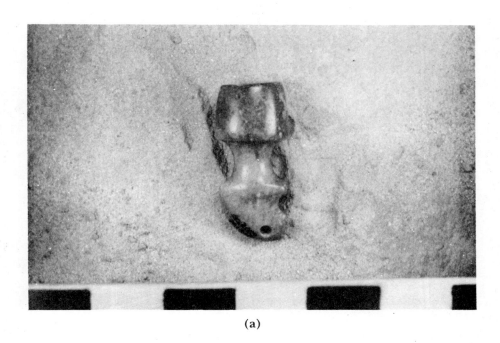

(a)

(b)

Figure 63. Keel-base bowl pipe of tan stone with perforated base. (a) Right side, showing perforation. (b) Near side of bowl, showing stem socket. From Ontario County, N. Y. RM 9079.

(a)

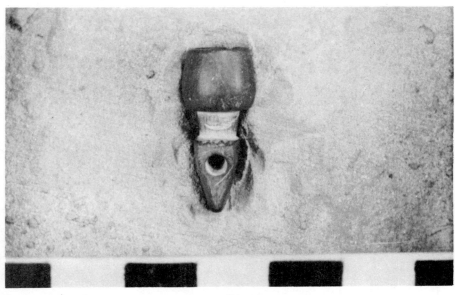

(b)

Figure 64. Keel-base bowl pipe of gray firestone or limestone. (a) View of near side of bowl, showing stem socket and damaged base, probably the result of a broken base perforation. (b) Right side. From Ontario County, N. Y. RM 25586.

(a)

(b)

Figure 65. Keel-base bowl pipe made of pottery. This example and that shown in Fig. 66 are pottery copies of the stone type. Such copies are rare but apparently do occur. The tan ware shows horizontal incised lines. (a) View into chamber orifice. (b) View showing near side, with socket, and right side, with perforation. From Dann site, Monroe County, N. Y. H. L. Schoff Collection, HFMAI 22/2954.

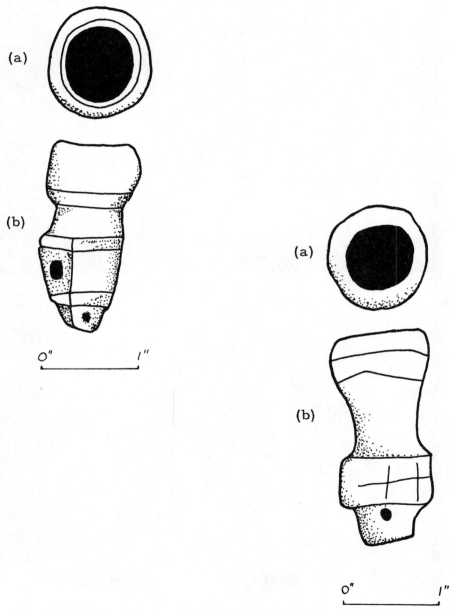

Figure 66. Keel-base bowl pipe of pottery (grayish black ware). The bowl and keel show incising, and the base is perforated. (a) View into chamber orifice. (b) Left side, showing base perforation. From Ontario County, N. Y. RM 25585.

BOWL-BASE PERFORATIONS
(Figs. 67–68)

Discussion

As I have already mentioned, the perforations found in the bases or spurs of the stone bowl pipes were probably used to secure the bowl to the removable, presumably wooden, stem by means of a fob. This use for the perforation makes it a functional design as well as being simply an aperture for hanging a decoration. As the end of the stem in the smoking chamber became charred and loosened through use, the smoker could then be reasonably assured that he would not lose the stem should it fall from the chamber. Stiles says that the Montagnais today use the fob in three ways: it connects the stem to the bowl; it serves as a colorful marker when the smoker loses the pipe in the snow (as happens often) ; and it functions as a holder for the hot bowl so that the Indian may whittle a new stem connection from the charred end of the one that has just fallen out (Stiles, personal communication, 1966) .

Figure 67 shows such a pipe, from the Smithsonian collection. Witthoft also supports this functional theory and uses the Montagnais as an example (Witthoft *et al.* 1953:90) . I was surprised to find that in my own family was an example of just such a type of decorative and functional pipe fob. Figure 68 shows the lower bowl and stem of a wooden pipe with silver inlay, made in Lindau, Germany, and smoked by the alpine herdsmen of Canton Appenzell, Switzerland. It is an example of parallel technologies, if not developments, in diverse cultures (W. E. Rutsch, personal communication, 1966) .

Figure 67. Keel-base bowl pipe with stem and fob. Bowl is made of a red catlinite-appearing stone, which probably comes from the Cree area's Lake Mistassini (Witthoft, personal communication, 1969). In the collection of the Heye Foundation Museum of the American Indian. Collected by Frank G. Speck from the Michikaman band of the Naskapi tribe, Labrador, Canada.

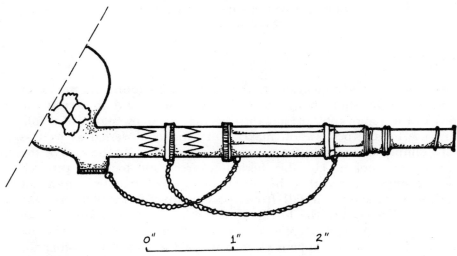

Figure 68. Stem of wooden pipe with silver inlay showing fob and chain connecting the stem and bowl. The removable stem is in two sections, both of which are connected to the bowl by chains. From Canton Appenzell, Switzerland, but made in Lindau, Germany. Collection of W. E. Rutsch.

CALUMET
(Figs. 69–72)

Physical Characteristics

Bar-base calumet pipe. This pipe bowl is generally made from one piece of stone; it consists of two rounded tubes that connect at a right angle at the elbow. The base continues forward in a forearm from the remote side of the bowl, tapering and ending within a short distance. The bowl is rounded, and the stem bore and the chamber meet at a right angle, as do the exterior surfaces. In several cases, it is difficult to distinguish between variations of the keel-base bowl pipe and those of the bar-base calumet pipe; however, the elongated bar base is diagnostic of the calumet type.

The pipe is usually of red pipestone or catlinite, a material imported from pipestone quarries in what is today Minnesota, South Dakota, and Wisconsin (Barber 1883:745). It is described as blood red with lighter red streaks and dots, compact, slatey, and able to receive a dull polish (Nicholet 1841:747).

Disk calumet pipe. Although this variety of calumet pipe also has the bar base, its disk-shaped bowl places it in another category. The bowl is a broad, flat disk with a shallow chamber in its center. The one example I have seen was described in the literature as constructed of "indurate fire clay" (see Fig. 71; Skinner 1926:39).

Discussion

The three examples that I saw of these calumet pipes which are presently attributable to identifiable sites have been dated to the Iroquoian Culture. Two of the six New York calumet pipes I examined were from sites in the Western Subarea; three were from the Central Subarea and one was from the Eastern Subarea. Ontario apparently has a richer store of this variety; I studied 10 calumet pipes from sites in the Neutral Area of Ontario, Canada. We can thus hypothesize only that these data show a preponderance in the Central Subarea of New York State and in the Neutral Area of Ontario, Canada, and that the calumet pipe is a late prehistoric and historic artifact.

The literature does not seem to contradict this hypothesis. Skinner mentions that the disk pipe was typical of the type found in Kansa and Osage Souian medicine bundles (Skinner 1926:39). The bar-base calumet type is comparable in shape to calumets from the Plains area that I have seen in numerous collections. The increased appearance of catlinite pipes in the Iroquois area after 1700 would tend to indicate a connection between the Iroquois and the Plains peoples (Wray 1956A:16). Not all calumet pipes are of catlinite, however; some are copies of the western calumets made of material available locally.

Ethnographic accounts of the eagle dance (calumet) rituals and the influx into the Northeast of western pipe styles and materials lead me to hypothesize again that the calumet ritual diffused into this area from the west in the late prehistoric or early historic period. It is very possible, from observations just made, that the Iroquois of western and central New York and of Ontario, Canada were affected by this diffusion to a greater degree than the Algonquian Indians further east.

Further study of calumet pipes and comparison with similar pipes from the entire Great Lakes and the Plains regions would be rewarding. It would be very interesting to discover what correlations could be made if enough examples from well-documented sites could be found.

Figure 69. Calumet pipe bowl of catlinite. From the grave of a Neutral Indian in the vicinity of Lake Medad, Ontario, Canada. L. J. Mullock and J. O. McGregor Collection, HFMAI 5/7024.

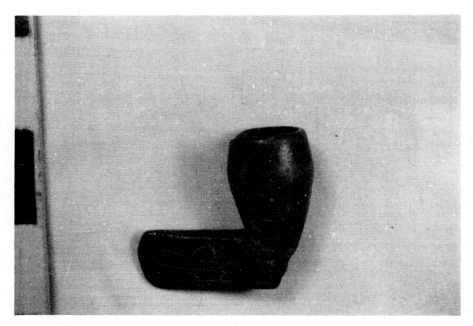

Figure 70. Calumet pipe bowl with keel-base bowl pipe features (bowl-keel portion is damaged). Possibly a transitional style between the keel-base bowl pipes and the bar-base bowl pipes. Brownish black mottled steatite with a polished exterior. Horizontal lines are incised laterally on the keel or base. From Grenadier Island, Jefferson County, N. Y. W. L. Pyle Collection, HFMAI 11/4382.

Figure 71. Disk-bowl calumet pipe of catlinite, with a mammal effigy in bas relief on the top of the disk. The "life line" extends from the mouth of the animal through its body. From Flamboro township, near Lake Medad, Ontario, Canada. (As illustrated in Skinner 1926:40, where scale is given as three-fourths the actual size.)

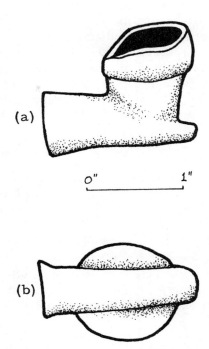

(a)

0"   1"

(b)

Figure 72. Bar-base bowl calumet pipe of black steatite with a distinct collar below the bowl rim. (a) Right side. (b) View of bottom. From South Dover, Dutchess County, N. Y. J. Wood Collection, HFMAI 15/7850.

Clay Pipes

PLAIN-BORE TUBE
(Figs. 73–74)

Physical Characteristics

As in the case of the stone tubes, I have classified what we assume to be smoking tubes of clay into two groups: plain-bore tubes and discrete-chambered tubes. The former are often called "cigar-shaped tubes," an appellation I consider inadequate because clay tubes appear to differ in internal, not necessarily external, construction. In the discrete-chambered tubes, the longer smoking material chamber is larger in diameter than is the shorter stem bore; in the plain-bore tube, a single chamber of constant diameter extends the entire length of the artifact (Ritchie 1965:252–57). Indeed, the exterior of the plain-bore clay tube varies in shape from cigarlike to bulbous or even vaselike. In New York State, however, this tube is usually cigar shaped and constructed of clay of local varieties, comparable to that used in the construction of Vinette I pottery (Ritchie 1965:193).

Discussion

We encounter the same problems outlined in the discussion of the plain-bore stone tubes: Was the plain-bore clay tube actually used as a pipe? For the same reasons given there, we shall assume it was. In fact, the plain-bore pottery tube, dated to the Early Woodland and Point Peninsula Cultures, has been suggested by Ritchie and Dragoo as the oldest pipe in the Northeast and a possible prototype for the stone tubes from the same period (Ritchie and Dragoo 1960:59; Ritchie 1965:193); in the Midwest, however, stone tubes are known to be older than their clay counterparts (Winters, personal communication, 1967).

This type of pipe is rare, and I was able to examine only one example personally (Fig. 73). Figure 74 is drawn from illustration in the literature. Therefore, I hesitate to hypothesize on either the culture or the geographical distribution of this type from my own data. The literature strongly supports a dating of Adenalike and Point Peninsula Cultures, and also gives a wide distribution for the limited number of examples found. Figures 73 and 74 illustrate the tubes from the

108

Morrow and Wray sites, respectively (both in the Central Subarea). Other plain-bore clay tubes have been reported from the Oberlander No. 2 site in Oswego County (also Central Subarea) and from the Muskalonge Lake site in Jefferson County (Northern Subarea). A fragment from the midden of the Riverhaven No. 2 site in Erie County (Western Subarea) is illustrated by Ritchie (Ritchie 1965: Plate 68, Fig. 4, 191). I have not included the plain-bore clay tubes in Tables 4 and 5 owing to scarcity of data.

Figure 73. Plain-bore pottery tube, undecorated. (a) **Right side.** (b) **Stem bore orifice. (c) Smoking chamber orifice. From the Morrow site, Ontario County, N. Y. H. Schoff Collection, RM 51010. (Also illustrated in Ritchie 1965:Plate 69, Fig. 5, 192.)**

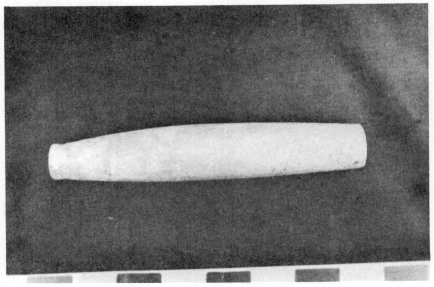

(a)

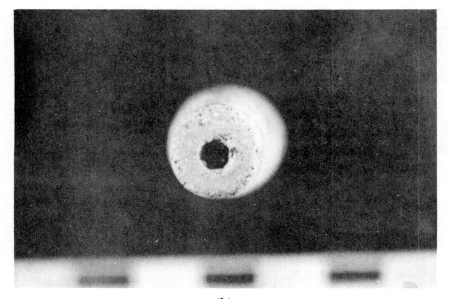

(b)

(c)

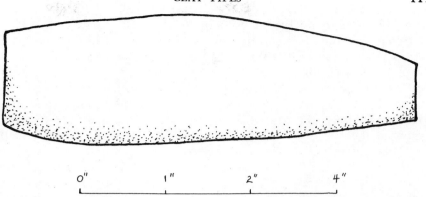

Figure 74. **Undecorated plain-bore pottery tube. From the Wray site, Monroe County, N. Y. On exhibit in the Rochester Museum. (As illustrated in Ritchie 1965:Plate 60, Fig. 15, 181.)**

DISCRETE-CHAMBERED TUBE
(Figs. 75–79)

Physical Characteristics

I have already defined the discrete-chambered tube as a tube in which the smoking material chamber and the stem bore have different diameters, the former being wider (and, incidentally, longer) than the latter. Like the plain-bore clay tubes, these pipes are often cigarlike in external appearance. They may also be conelike, with the stem-bore end tapered, and are usually constructed of local clays with a fine grit or sand temper, although researchers have found great variation in composition and quality.

The discrete-chambered clay tubes are reported to be usually undecorated, although Figs. 75 and 76 both show incised decoration. One type of this tube is, as Ritchie calls it, a notable exception—that is, the example from the Wickham Point site, the outer surface of which is covered with protrusions termed "mammillary bosses" (Fig. 77). Ritchie suggests that the bosses may have been intended as representations of the kernels on an ear of corn (Ritchie 1965:265).

Discussion

I examined three tubes having discrete chambers, two of which were from sites in the Central Subarea and could be dated to the Point Peninsula Culture, which, according to the literature, is possible, although these pipes are generally identified as Owasco (Ritchie 1965:295). The first examples are found in the Hunter's Home Phase of the Point Peninsula Culture and are considered the prototypes of later pipes (Ritchie 1965:254, 295).

I have included two other pipes of the mammillary boss variety from the literature with my illustrations of the discrete-chambered tube because of their distinctive style. Figure 78 shows what we might call an incipient obtuse-angle pipe, the bend being very slight. It is from the White site in Chenango County and is attributed to the Hunter's Home Phase of the Point Peninsula Culture. Figure 79 shows a definite obtuse-angle mammillary boss pipe from the Hilltop site; it is attributable to the Owasco Culture, as is another such pipe from the Lakeside Park site in Cayuga County. Ritchie interprets these findings to illustrate the continuity between the Point Peninsula and Owasco Cultures (Ritchie 1965:254). They may also be indicative of a developmental trend in clay pipes from the tube to the obtuse angle. In either case, the pipes showing the mammillary boss motif deserve mention here.

Again, the uses of the tube for smoking are hypothetical. The discrete-chambered tube may be an improvement over the plain-bore tube because it allows the smoker to tamp his smoking mixture into his pipe without having it fall from the stem end. Yet we would suppose that the stone platform pipe of the same period would do this job better because of its sharp angle between the smoking chamber and the stem bore.

Figure 75. Discrete-chambered clay tube with a conelike shape, tapering at the stem-bore end. Lightly incised tan ware with double lines enclosing a band of incised rectangular decorations. (a) Side view. (b) Smoking chamber orifice. (c) Photograph of side. From the Bell-Philhower site in Sussex County, N. J. RM AR 40280.

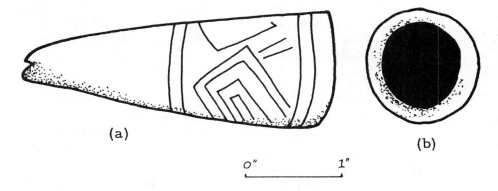

(a)

(b)

0"   1"

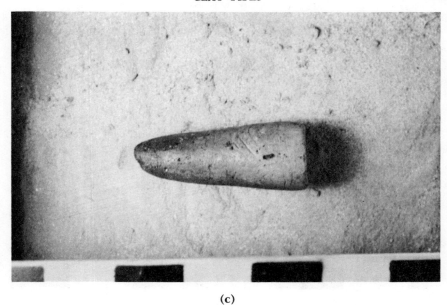

(c)

Figure 76. Discrete-chambered clay tube with a general bulbous shape, narrowing at the stem-bore end. Dark tan ware with two rows of short incised lines encircling the rim of the smoking material chamber. (a) Stem bore end. (b) Right side. (c) Smoking material chamber orifice. From the Wickham site, Oswego County, N. Y. RM 38454 (Rochester field notes of August 28, 1943).

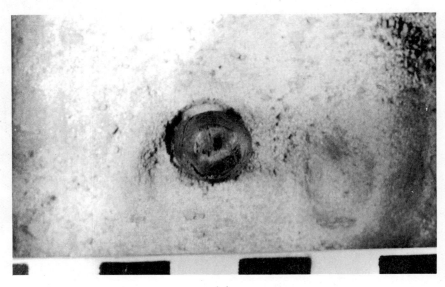

(a)

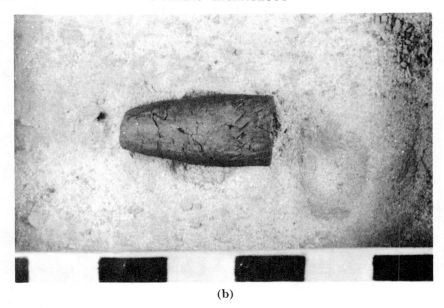

(b)

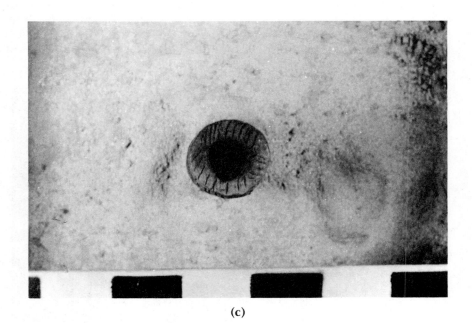

(c)

Figure 77. Discrete-chambered clay tube of dark brown ware. Stem bore is unfinished. The exterior is covered almost to the bit with mammillary bosses, which are separated from the smooth band around the bit end by a row of short incised lines. (a) Right side. (b) Smoking material chamber orifice. From the Wickham site, Oswego County, N. Y. RM (on display).

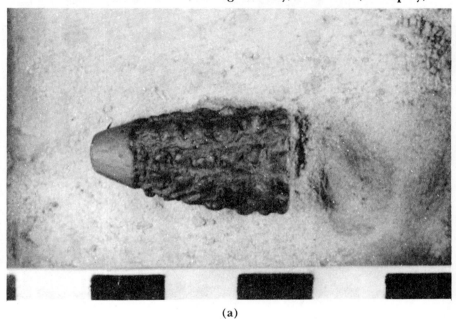

(a)

(b)

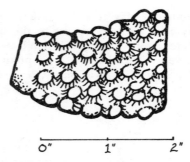

Figure 78. Discrete-chambered clay tube with slight curvature, possibly the beginning of the obtuse-angle style. The view is of the right side. The exterior is almost entirely covered by mammillary bosses. From the White site in Chenango County, N. Y. (As illustrated in Ritchie 1965:Plate 87, Fig. 22, 256.)

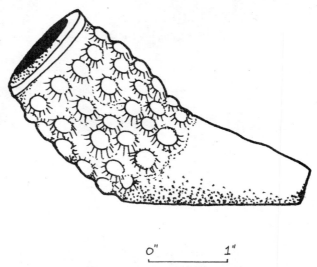

Figure 79. Obtuse-angle clay pipe, left side tilted slightly to show the rim and bowl orifice. The bowl is covered to the elbow and heel with mammillary bosses. The stem is undecorated. From the Hilltop site, Delaware County, N. Y. (As illustrated in Ritchie 1965:Plate 100, Fig. 4, 294.)

SIMPLE OBTUSE ANGLE
(Figs. 80–96)

Physical Characteristics

Like the obtuse-angle stone pipes, obtuse-angle clay pipes are those pipes having an elbow angle of more than 90 and less than 180 degrees. Unlike its stone counterpart, however, this classification of clay artifact contains by far the greatest number of clay pipes of numerous and diverse styles. Indeed, all the following types we shall discuss fall into the obtuse-angle category, and are therefore really subclassifications: basket bowl; ring bowl; trumpet bowl; square-collared bowl; escutcheon; effigy (human, mammal, bird, open mouth, reptile and amphibian) ; and miscellaneous obtuse angle, the catch-all of all those examples that do not meet my arbitrary specifications for the other types.

Because the basic construction of these types is similar, I have differentiated them by bowl shape or bowl decoration, which I consider to be the most distinguishing feature among these artifacts. As far as I have been able to determine, pipestems have not lent themselves to analysis as diagnostic of a typology. Some pottery pipes have a distinctive bit, which may have resulted from use or may have been modeled by the maker.

What I term "simple obtuse-angle clay pipes," then, are those examples that show no bowl differentiation, and carry no, or very rudimentary, decoration. The rim of the bowl may be occasionally pronounced or decorated (Figs. 80, 91–92, 95–96) or lightly incised (Figs. 93–94). The stem and bowl of this "simple" variety maintain predominantly straight sides, and although several examples have lateral stem ridges (Figs. 80–84, 86) and flattened bases, the generally straight "lines" of this type remain undisturbed. These pipes are constructed of local clays and examples vary widely in quality and temper.

Discussion

I was able to study 31 simple obtuse-angle pipes that were identifiable by culture: 7, Point Peninsula; 19, Owasco; and 5, Iroquoian. In no other type is there such a wide distribution among cultures. A geographical breakdown of pipes studied yields a larger group with identifiable provenience: 1, Western Subarea; 29, Central Subarea; 8, Northern Subarea; 13, Ontario (12 from the Neutral area and 1 from the St. Lawrence area). Six were of unknown provenience, other than New York State.

The position of this type in the development of pipes between the Owasco Culture and that in which the five Iroquoian tribes emerged is unclear. Owing to this gap in the archaeological chronology between the Owasco people and the prehistoric five Iroquois tribes, no clearcut breakdown of Owasco pipe types has been possible. The flattened bases and lateral ridges of the simple obtuse-angle pipe may indicate a vestigial link to the platform pipes of stone of an earlier culture. At any rate, the type cannot now be documented beyond culture; when the phase is known, perhaps it can be classified in a typology by criteria other than those of physical appearance.

Figure 80. Obtuse-angle pipe of black ware with distinct rim and incised lateral stem ridges. (a) Left side, tilted to show left and center ridges. (b) View into smoking chamber orifice. From Levanna, Cayuga County, N. Y. RM (number illegible).

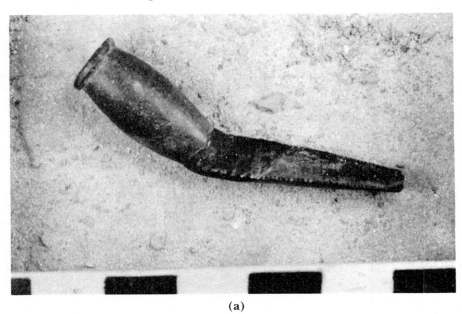

(a)

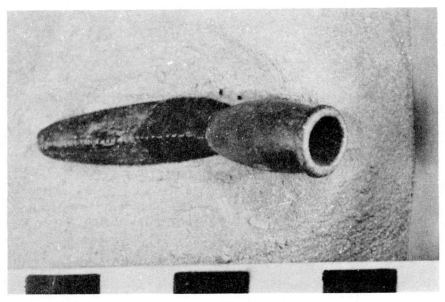

(b)

Figure 81. Obtuse-angle pipe of rough-tempered tan ware, with lateral ridges along the stem and bowl. (a) Right side. (b) Smoking chamber orifice. From the Hunter's Home site, Wayne County, N. Y. Collection in the Cayuga Museum, Auburn, N. Y.

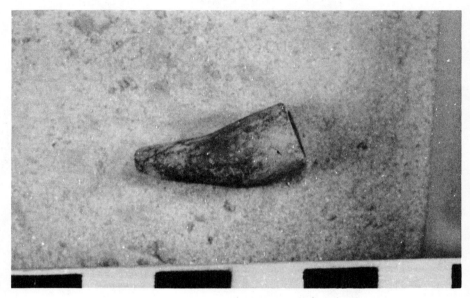

(a)

(b)

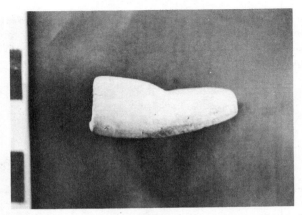

Figure 82. Obtuse-angle pipe of tan ware with flattened lateral ridges and a slight central ridge along the stem and bowl. From Aylmer, Elgin County, Ontario, Canada. HFMAI 6/6767.

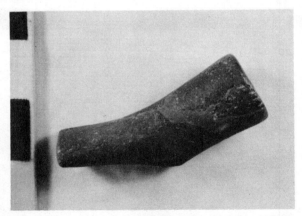

Figure 83. View of right side of obtuse-angle pipe, partially restored, of dark tan ware and with lateral stem ridges. From Union Springs, Cayuga County, N. Y. HFMAI 4/5527.

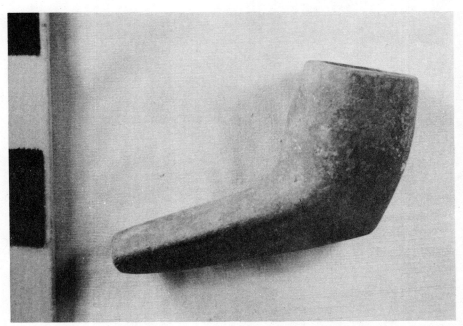

Figure 84. View of right side of obtuse-angle pipe of tan ware with lateral stem ridges and a ridge extending between them around the heel of the bowl. From St. Joseph's, Cayuga County, N. Y. HFMAI /3192.

Figure 85. Partially restored obtuse-angle pipe of tan ware. (a) Right side. (b) View into smoking chamber orifice. From the Sackett site, Ontario County, N. Y. RM (number illegible).

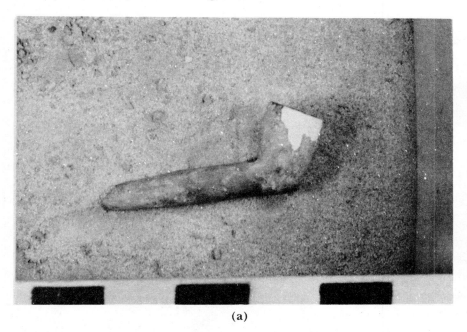

(a)

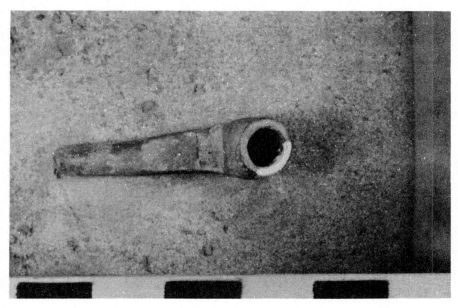

(b)

Figure 86. Obtuse-angle pipe of black ware with distinct rim and lateral stem ridges curving under the elbow toward, and meeting at, the heel. (a) Right side. (b) View into smoking chamber orifice. From the Sackett site, Ontario County, N. Y. RM 2733.

(a)

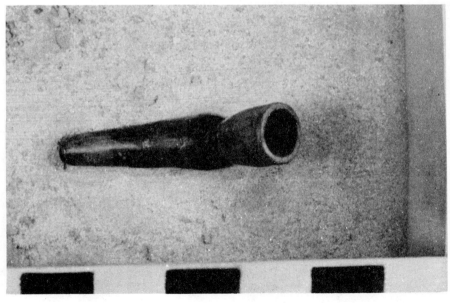

(b)

Figure 87. Undecorated obtuse-angle pipe of red ware. (a) **Right side.** (b) **View from above, into smoking chamber orifice. From Rome, Oneida County, N. Y. RM 20369.**

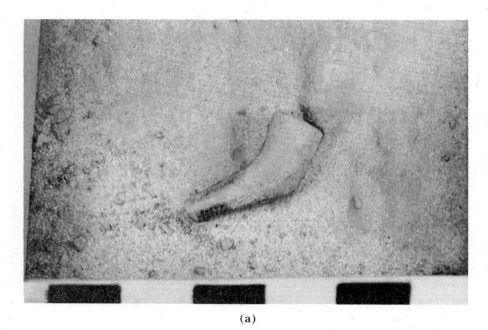

(a)

(b)

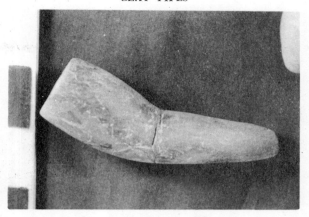

Figure 88. Undecorated obtuse-angle pipe of tan ware. From Union Springs, Cayuga County, N. Y. HFMAI 9/4498.

Figure 89. Undecorated obtuse-angle pipe of black ware. (a) Right side of pipe, showing long stem and slight bit definition. (b) View into smoking chamber orifice. From Cayuga County, N. Y. RM 10125.

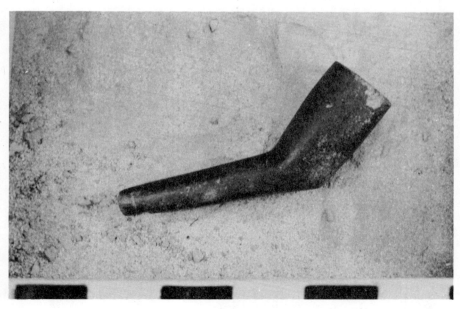

(a)

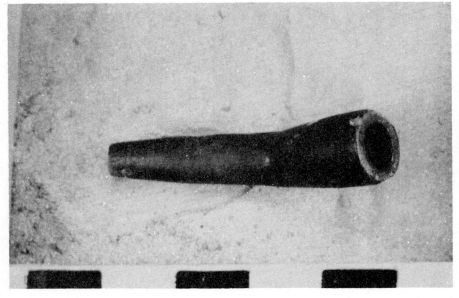

(b)

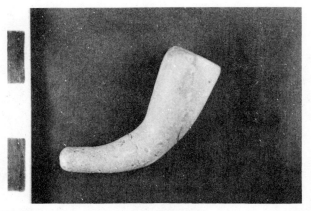

Figure 90. Undecorated obtuse-angle pipe of tan ware, right side. From Oneida County, N. Y. HFMAI 4/8596.

Figure 91. Obtuse-angle pipe of tan ware with lopsided, slightly flared rim. (a) View showing top of stem and smoking chamber orifice. (b) Right side, tilted to show smoking chamber orifice. From the Tomlin Farm, town of Rutland, Jefferson County, N. Y. RM 20355.

(a)

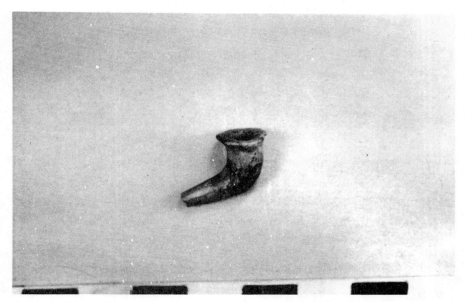

(b)

Figure 92. Obtuse-angle pipe of tan ware with distinct rim. (a) **Right side.** (b) View of stem top, showing smoking chamber orifice. **From Phelp's Farm, town of Adams, Jefferson County, N. Y. RM 20357.**

(a)

(b)

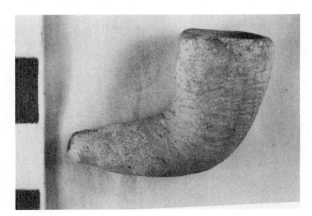

Figure 93. Obtuse-angle pipe of tan ware with incised lines on the bottom of the stem and on the remote side of the bowl. **From Troy, Rensselaer County, N. Y. HFMAI 20/4032.**

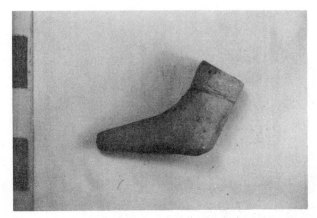

Figure 94. Obtuse-angle pipe of brown ware. **One incised line encircles the rim, and an incised "X" appears above the line on the right side of the bowl. From Storrs Harbor, Jefferson County, N. Y. HFMAI /9889.**

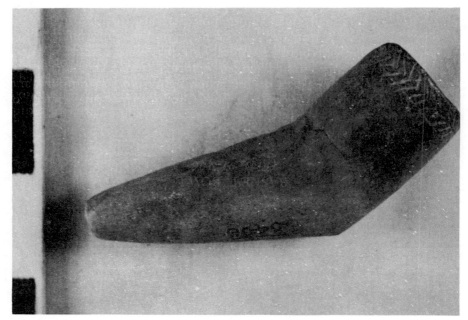

Figure 95. Obtuse-angle pipe of tan ware with two rows of incised lines forming a chevron pattern around the rim. From Farley's Point, Cayuga County, N. Y. HFMAI 8/8408.

Figure 96. Obtuse-angle pipe of tan ware with a row of heavily incised chevronlike lines directly below the rim edge, under which appears an incised line and a row of punctates encircling the bowl. (a) View into smoking chamber orifice, showing two circular rows of incising around the orifice. (b) Right side of pipe. Note that the stem has been repaired. From the Burning Springs site, Cattaraugus County, N. Y. RM 17584.

(a)

(b)

BASKET BOWL
(Figs. 97–106)

Physical Characteristics

I have used the term "basket bowl" to describe this variety of obtuse-angle clay pipe because the shape of its bowl is bulbous and bulges, as does a full, circular basket. Figure 97 shows an undecorated basket-bowl pipe, but most examples I studied were extensively decorated. Variations within the type occur. The punctates on Fig. 103 may show an incipient effigy. Most, however, are distinguishable by the rim style: wide, ridged collar (Figs. 99, 105–106); raised and/or constricted collars (Figs. 101–104). Some examples show only slight bulging (Fig. 100), but are distinctive enough to be classified under the basket-bowl heading and not miscellaneous. The basket-bowl pipe is made of a wide variety of locally available clays.

Discussion

I could identify 21 of the pipes I studied by culture: 18, Owasco; 3, Iroquoian. Twenty-two examples were attributable to subareas: 21, Central Subarea; 1, Northern Subarea. One pipe could be identified only as New York State, and I examined no examples from Canada.

From these data, a postulation of Owasco and possibly early Iro-quoian is possible for the basket-bowl pipe. The heavy concentration in the Central Subarea proves inconclusive when we take into account Lenig's research of this type in the Eastern Subarea (Lenig 1965). It may well be that the basket-bowl variety is an incipient type that developed into the traditional pipes of the Iroquois tribes of the Eastern Subarea.

Figure 97. **Basket-bowl pipe of gray ware. View shown is of stem top (note stem repair and distinct rim) and smoking chamber orifice. From the Sackett site, Ontario County, N. Y. RM 27700.**

Figure 98. (a) Right side of basket-bowl pipe of tan ware. Vertical rows
.of chevronlike incised lines encircle the bowl. Vertically incised lines encircle the rim. (b) View of stem top and smoking chamber orifice. From the
Partridge site, Chenango County, N. Y. RM 29319.

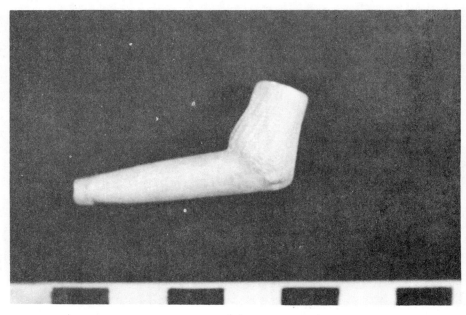

(a)

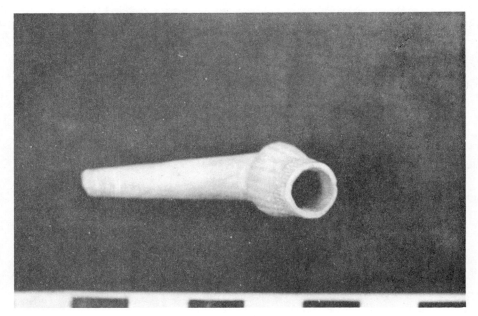

(b)

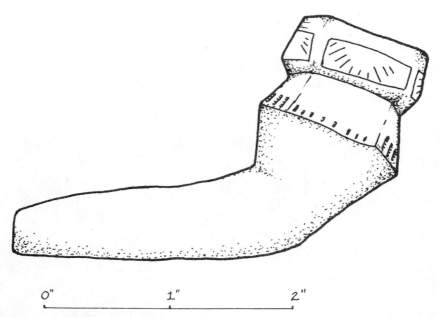

Figure 99. Right side basket-bowl pipe with bulbar, flared bowl, geometrically indented so as to separate the lower bowl from the wide collar. Vertical ridges on the collar form its corners. Collar shows light incising and punctates, and a row of punctates appears just above the indentation at the widest part of the bowl. From the Winney Island site, Saratoga County, N. Y. Collected by Anthony Sassi of Corinth, N. Y. No. WI V. 205.

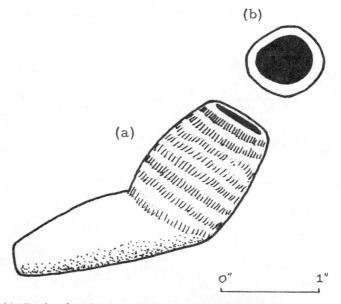

Figure 100. Basket-bowl pipe of brown ware with parallel rows of short incised marks (perhaps made by a cord-wrapped paddle) encircling the entire bowl. (a) Right side. (b) Smoking chamber orifice. From a grave in the town of Moravia, Onondaga County. HFMAI 5/3707.

Figure 101. Basket-bowl pipe of tan ware with a constricted rim. The bulbar portion of the bowl is encircled by an incised zigzag line, and incised lines encircle the rim with punctate marks in the incising. (a) Right side. (b) Smoking chamber orifice. From the Sackett site, Ontario County, N. Y. RM 27715.

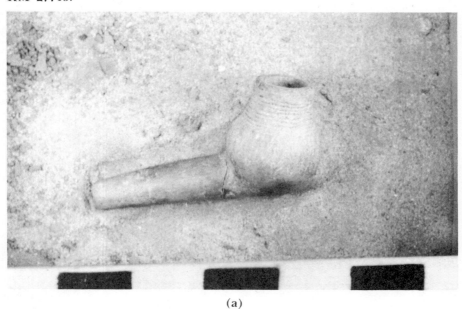

(a)

(b)

Figure 102. Basket-bowl pipe of tan ware showing rim constriction below a slightly flared collar. The bowl is decorated with vertical, slanting, incised lines, with a vertical row of punctates every fifth line. The collar shows horizontal rows of incising and punctates. From the Ellisburg site, Jefferson County, N. Y. RM 19382.

Figure 103. Basket-bowl pipe of tan ware with bulbar bowl constricted below rim to form raised collar, decorated by horizontal rows of incised lines. Four groups of vertical incised lines are found around the bowl, with a triangular punctate pattern (perhaps suggesting a face, and, therefore, a rudimentary effigy?) on the right, left, and remote sides of the bowl. (a) Right side. (b) View into smoking chamber orifice. From the **Partridge** site, Chenango County, N. Y. RM 29318.

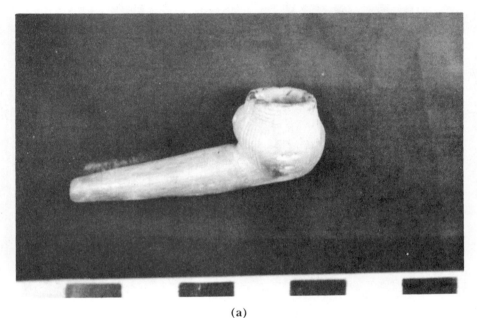

(a)

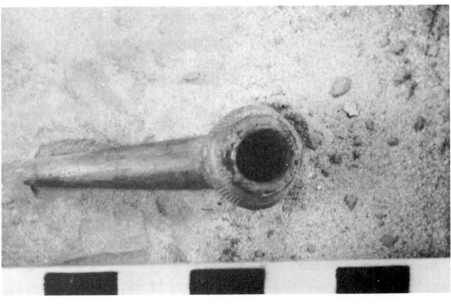

(b)

Figure 104. Basket-bowl pipe of tan ware. The bowl is surmounted by a very high collar, seen in view (a), the right side. One row of vertical incising on the rim appears above tight, horizontal, parallel, incised lines encircling the collar. The bowl shows vertical rows of incised lines interspersed with rows of incised chevrons and punctates. (b) View into smoking chamber orifice. From A. L. Hopkins' Farm, Cayuga County, N. Y. RM 7082.

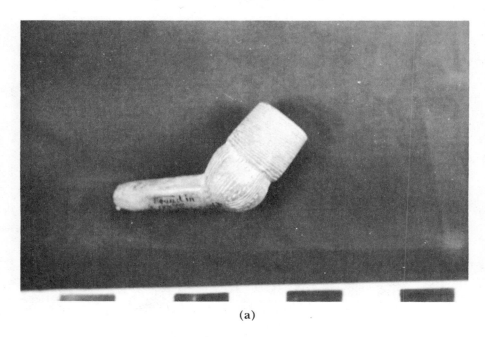

(a)

(b)

Figure 105. Basket-bowl pipe of tan ware. The bowl is indented above the elbow and again below the rim, the latter indentation forming a high collar area. The collar is hexagonal, especially obvious in the view of the smoking chamber orifice (a), and is decorated by four, slanted, incised grooves interspersed with a similarly slanted row of punctates repeated on each of the six sides. (b) Right side. The bowl portion is undecorated. From the Morse Farm, Jefferson County, N. Y. RM 20577.

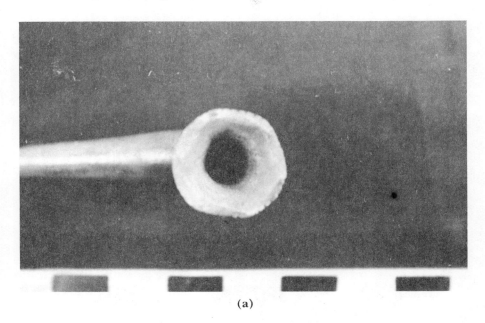

(a)

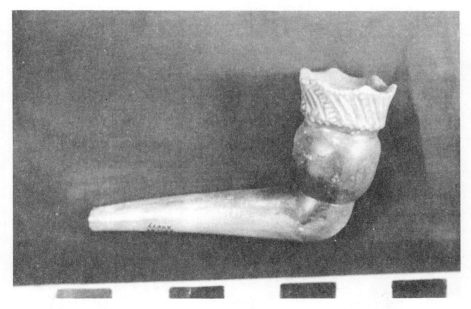

(b)

Figure 106. Obtuse-angle clay pipe of tan ware with slightly bulbous bowl surmounted by a heavily incised pentagonal collar. The bowl beneath the collar is also incised, to the point where rings have formed. One row of punctates encircles the bowl beneath the rings. View (a) shows the smoking chamber orifice and the pentagonal shape of the rim. (b) Right side. The pipe is included here mainly for its close resemblance to Fig. 105. From the Morse Farm, Jefferson County, N. Y. RM 20571.

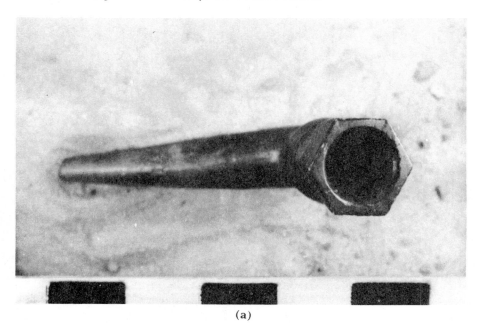

(a)

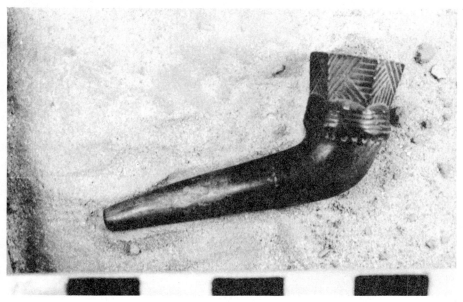

(b)

RING BOWL
(Figs. 107–121)

Physical Characteristics

I have chosen the term "ring bowl" to describe the classification of obtuse-angle pipe the characteristic feature of which is horizontally incised and/or punctate lines encircling the bowl and separated from each other far enough apart so that a rounded coil-like "ring" of clay has been formed between them. This description, of course, is of the "classic" form; variations are numerous, and I have included in my study several pipes without the definite "rings" described simply because they resemble the ring-bowl pipes in their general construction and bowl shape. We should note that the ring-bowl pipe has been described in the literature both as an "elbow pipe" (many examples have a sharp angle at the elbow of close to 90 degrees) and as an "acorn-bowl pipe."

The subtypes of the ring-bowl classification are again distinguished by bowl features. I have divided the pipes into two main groups: the predominantly straight-sided ring-bowl pipe and the predominantly bulbar ring-bowl pipe. The straight-sided category includes pipes with narrow bowls—that is, the circumference changes little from the elbow to the rim—and pipes with gently flared bowls—that is, the circumference at the rim is greater than that at the elbow. The bulbar group includes those pipes termed "acorn bowl" in the literature. The decoration of the ring-bowl pipe varies widely, as the illustrations indicate, but follows the general pattern of horizontal rows of incised lines, punctates, and/or rings.

Discussion

Of the 102 ring-bowl pipes I was able to examine personally, 31 originated from sites identifiable by culture: 30, Iroquoian; 1, Point Peninsula. These data support the case for this style being an Iroquoian marker. The one odd pipe may represent that random datum that it is not pertinent—that is, providing it is not substantiated by future research.

Geographical distribution was heaviest in the Central Subarea with 34 examples; 5 were from the Western Subarea and 1 each was attributed to the Southern, Northern, and Eastern Subareas. Fifty-eight examples were attributable to Ontario, Canada, with 56 from the Neutral area and 1 each from the Huronia and Saint Lawrence areas. Two were of unknown provenience other than New York State.

The only relevant factor from this distribution would seem to be a high incidence of the type in the Central Subarea and the Neutral area of Ontario; however, as I have stated previously, we must remember that the museum collections I used probably contain more artifacts from these areas than from the others.

Several students have suggested to me that the variations between straight-sided ring-bowl pipes and bulbar ring-bowl pipes are diagnostic of straight-sided pipes on earlier sites and bulbar pipes on later sites. For the following analysis, I discarded those examples that were not obviously straight sided or obviously bulbar. I also discarded the 58 examples from Ontario, because I felt that there was less chance of identifying them to a provenience smaller than the areas mentioned. I divided the 42 remaining pipes, those from New York State with distinct ring-bowl features as defined, into two groups, 21 each in the straight-sided and bulbar categories. All 42 were classified as historical Iroquoian artifacts. I could not carry out the analysis further inasmuch as a complete chronology has not yet been devised for the site. On the Boughton Hill site, both styles appear, with 8 straight-sided pipes and 6 bulbar examples. Both styles also occur on the Dann site in Monroe County, with 11 straight sided and 3 bulbar.

On the chance that a geographical distribution might occur, I plotted the data as follows:

Style	Subarea			
	Western	Central	Northern	Eastern
Straight sided	1	16	3	1
Bulbar	4	15	1	1

From these data I can only conclude that as far as my research goes, the two styles of ring-bowl obtuse-angle pipe are geographically and chronologically contemporaneous. Further refinement of the exact archaeological and geographical position of each site may disprove this conclusion, as well may a less subjective method of assigning ring-bowl pipes to either category.

Figure 107. (a) Right side of straight-sided ring-bowl pipe of tan ware. Closely parallel incised lines are enclosed between two larger horizontal rows of punctates, one on the rim and the other midway between the elbow and the rim. One incised groove larger than its neighbors occurs directly below the punctate rim. (b) View of stem top and smoking chamber orifice. From the Morse Farm, Watertown, Jefferson County, N. Y. RM 25632.

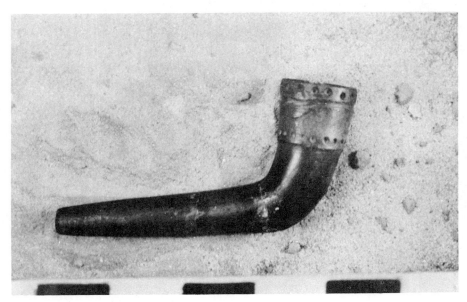

(a)

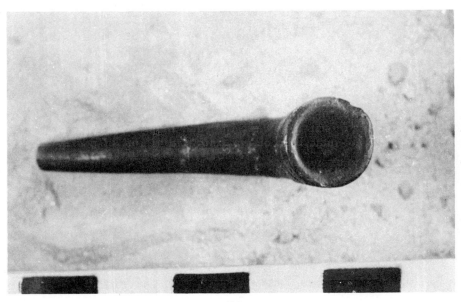

(b)

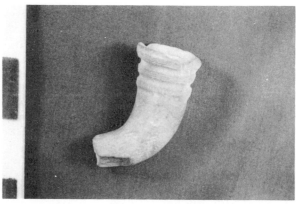

Figure 108. Straight-sided ring-bowl pipe of black to dark brown ware. View of right side shows bowl damage and broken stem. Closely parallel incised lines ring the rim, under which is found, in order from top to bottom, a deep incised groove, another band of closely parallel incised lines, another deep incised groove, and a row of vertical incised lines also encircling the bowl. From Fleming, Cayuga County, N. Y. D. Cadgow Collection, HFMAI 13/2178.

Figure 109. Straight-sided ring-bowl pipe of gray ware, showing one row of punctates encircling the bowl at its widest point. From Boughton Hill site, Victor, Ontario County, N. Y. H. L. Schoff Collection, HFMAI 22/3311.

Figure 110. Straight-sided ring-bowl pipe of tan ware, fitted with a copper mouthpiece. View of right side shows the three incised lines encircling the bowl at its widest point. From the Dann site, Monroe County, N. Y. H. L. Schoff Collection, HFMAI 22/2937.

Figure 111. Straight-sided ring-bowl pipe of tan ware. (a) Smoking chamber orifice. (b) Right side, showing three incised lines encircling the widest part of the bowl. From the McClure site, Canandaigua, Ontario County, N. Y. RM 18683.

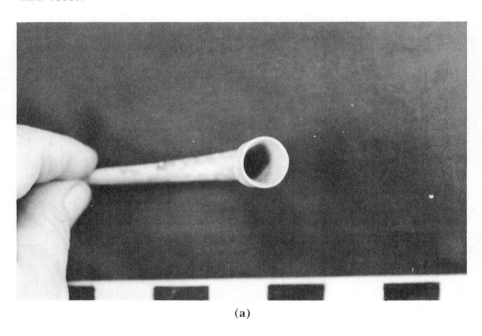

(a)

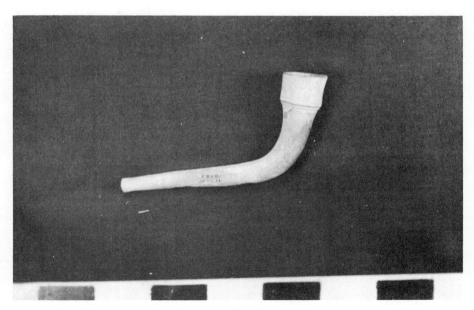

(b)

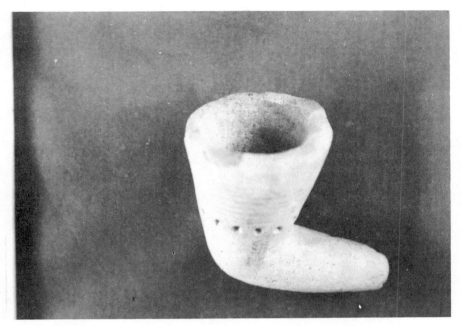

Figure 112. Straight-sided ring-bowl pipe with flared bowl, of reddish tan ware. View is of left side, showing incised parallel lines encircling three-quarters of the bowl starting at the rim. One row of punctates encircles the bowl beneath the rings. From Chautauqua County, N. Y. HFMAI 11/4533.

Figure 113. Straight-sided ring-bowl pipe of tan ware with flared bowl. Incised parallel lines encircle the bowl. From Erie County, N. Y. George J. Riebuhr Collection, HFMAI 16/3270.

Figure 114. Straight-sided, flared, ring-bowl pipe of reddish tan ware. Incised, parallel rings cover three-quarters of the bowl from the rim. One ring of punctates encircles the bowl below the last incised line. (a) Smoking chamber orifice. (b) Right side. From Great Gully site, Cayuga County, N. Y. RM 20458.

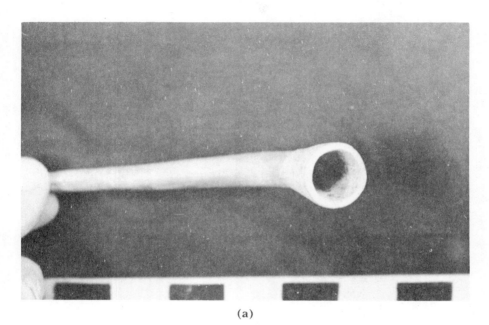

(a)

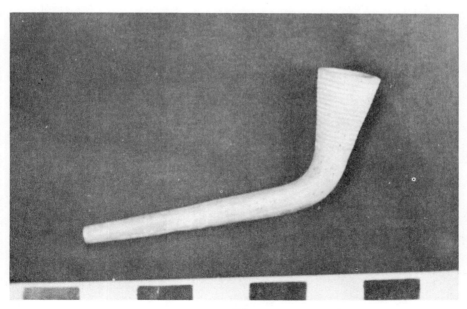

(b)

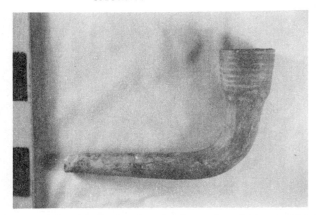

Figure 115. Straight-sided ring-bowl pipe of tan ware. Right side view shows evenly spaced rings encircling the bowl, formed by relatively wide incised grooves. One row of diagonal punctates appears below the bottom ring. From the Dann site, Monroe County, N. Y. H. L. Schoff Collection, HFMAI 22/2942.

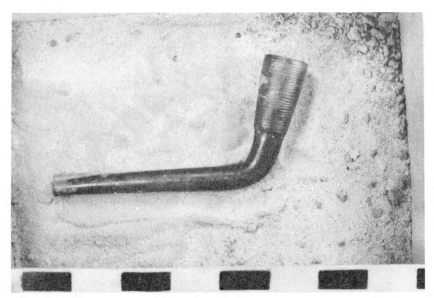

Figure 116. Straight-sided, flared, ring-bowl pipe of black ware. Right side view shows very closely spaced rings covering the bowl, formed by incised lines. One row of widely spaced punctates occurs below the last ring. From Great Gully site, Cayuga County, N. Y. RM 20465.

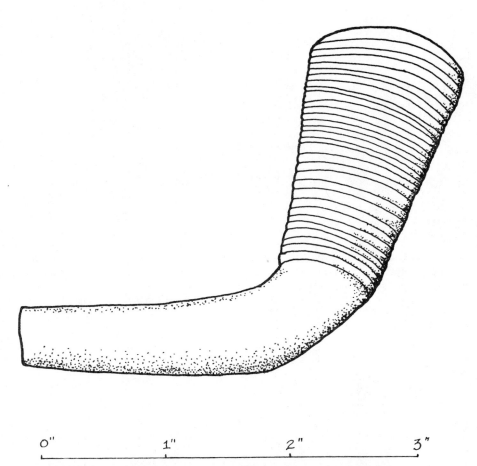

Figure 117. Right side of straight-sided, flared, ring-bowl pipe. Rows of incised lines encircle the bowl forming rings. From Winney Island site, Saratoga County, N. Y. Collection of Anthony Sassi, Corinth, N. Y. No. WI V. 406.

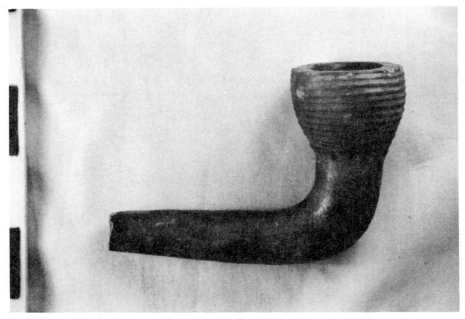

Figure 118. Right side of bulbar ring-bowl pipe, slightly tilted so that the smoking chamber orifice is visible. Tan ware. Horizontal and parallel incised lines and rings encircle the bowl; one row of punctates appears beneath the rings. From the Neutral village of Kienuka, four miles east of Lewiston, Niagara County, N. Y. W. J. Mackay Collection, HFMAI 8/8538.

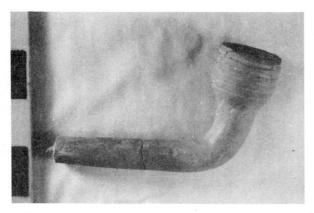

Figure 119. Bulbar ring-bowl pipe of tan ware. Incising circles the chamber orifice, and horizontal and parallel incised lines form rings around the bowl. One row of oblong punctates encircles the bowl beneath the rings. From the Boughton Hill site, Ontario County, N. Y. H. L. Schoff Collection, HFMAI 22/3305.

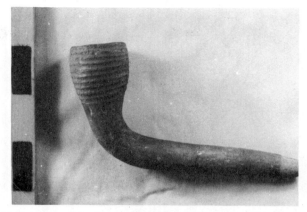

Figure 120. Left side of bulbar ring-bowl pipe of red to tan ware. Horizontal and parallel raised rings encircle the bowl, separated by wide, incised grooves. One row of diagonally slanted punctates appears below the rings. From the Dann site, Monroe County, N. Y. H. L. Schoff Collection, HFMAI 22/2945.

Figure 121. Bulbar ring-bowl pipe of tan ware. (a) Smoking chamber orifice. (b) Right side. Punctates and incising circle the chamber orifice. The ringed bowl shows a row of punctates below the last ring. From Green Lake, Orchard Park, Erie County, N. Y. RM 17625.

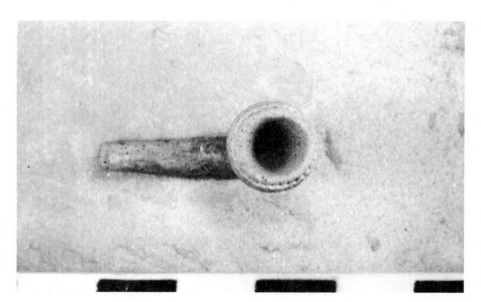

(a)

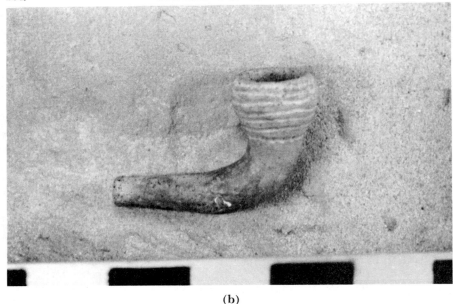

(b)

TRUMPET
(Figs. 122–136)

Physical Characteristics

Many obtuse-angle pipes lend themselves to classification by rim shape as well as bowl shape; an example is the trumpet pipe, in which the bowl rim is greatly flared and thus resembles a cornet or even a squash blossom. This type can be decorated or undecorated and occurs in numerous varieties and materials; therefore, subclassification is difficult. However, Pendergast has subdivided trumpet pipes into two subgroups with which I can concur: those with a flared rim he labels "trumpet"; those without a flared rim—that is, those with a flared bowl —he calls "modified trumpet" (Pendergast 1966:Fig. 289, 197).

Discussion

I have examined and recorded a total of 103 pipes of the trumpet variety. Of these, 20 were attributed to sites identifiable by culture: 16, Iroquoian; 4, Owasco. Geographical distribution follows: 28, Northern Subarea; 10, Southern Subarea; 6, Western Subarea; 3, Eastern Subarea. No trumpet pipes were from the Southern Subarea, and 4 had provenience known only as New York State. Ontario was represented in my sample by 48 examples from the Neutral area and 4 from Huronia.

These data have led me to generalize that the trumpet pipe is probably an Iroquoian artifact, perhaps having developmental roots in the Owasco. Geographical data may indicate that this style was popular in the Northern Subarea; further analysis may show the trumpet pipe to be a distinctive artifact in the Northern Subarea and in Ontario.

Figure 122. **Trumpet pipe of brown ware with slightly flared bowl. (a) Smoking chamber orifice. (b) Right side. From the Calligan Farm, Rutland, Jefferson County, N. Y. RM 20336.**

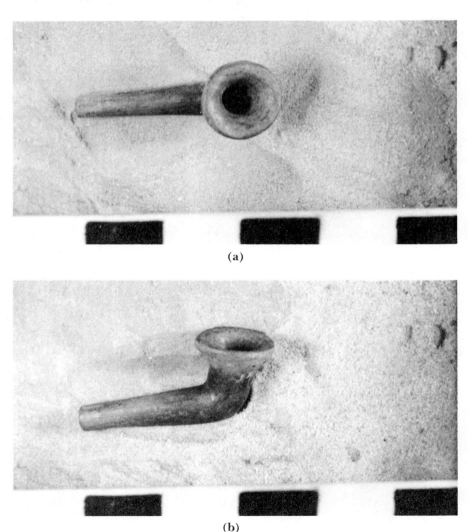

(a)

(b)

Figure 123. (a) Right side of tan ware trumpet pipe with slightly flared bowl. (b) Smoking chamber orifice. From Normander Farm, Rutland, Jefferson County, N. Y. RM 20364.

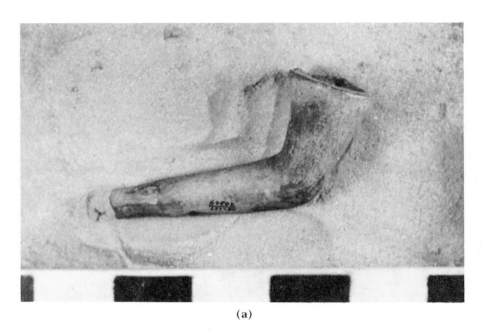

(a)

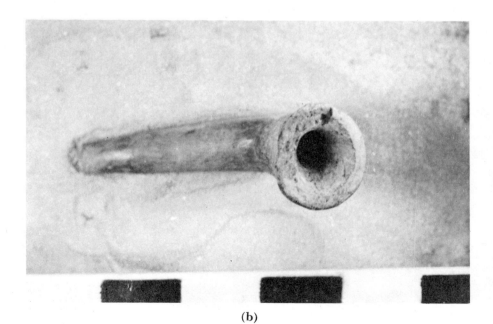

(b)

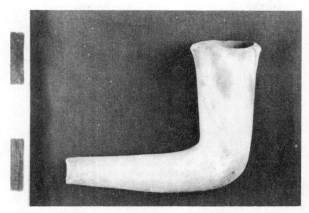

Figure 124. Trumpet pipe of reddish tan ware with a long bowl and a slightly flared rim. From Cooperstown, Oswego County, N. Y. HFMAI 20/4033.

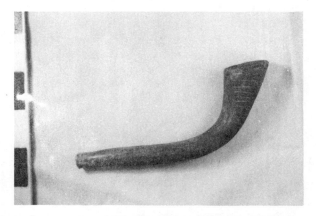

Figure 125. Trumpet pipe of gray ware with flared bowl decorated by incised lines parallel and horizontal to the rim. From the Boughton Hill site, Victor, Ontario County, N. Y. H. L. Schoff Collection, HFMAI 22/3310. (Note the similarity to several of the ring-bowl pipes. Again, the distinctions between types are often arbitrary and are certainly not absolute.)

Figure 126. View of right side of trumpet pipe of black ware with a flared bowl. "V"-shaped incised lines and punctates encircle the bowl (not visible). From E. Young's farm, Union Springs, Cayuga County, N. Y. HFMAI 19/9789.

Figure 127. Trumpet pipe with flared, decorated bowl, of tan ware. (a) Smoking chamber orifice. (b) Right side, showing two bands of vertical incising, which occur on either side of horizontal and parallel incised lines forming a band, in the center of which occurs a wide groove. The stem has been damaged. From the Nichols Pond site, Madison County, N. Y. RM 19279.

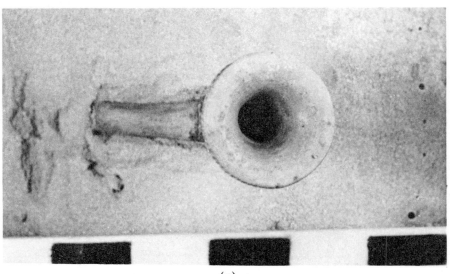

(a)

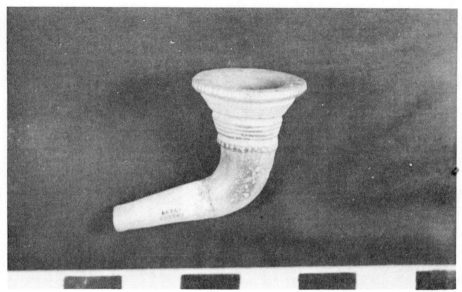

(b)

Figure 128. Trumpet pipe of tan ware with flared rim. A row of vertical incising circles the rim, and the bowl is covered with horizontal incising, under which appears a row of punctates. From Otsego County, N. Y. HFMAI 4/2485.

Figure 129. Left side of trumpet pipe of tan ware with flared rim and broken stem. From Perch River, Jefferson County, N. Y. A. A. Getman Collection, HFMAI /9881.

Figure 130. Trumpet pipe of brown ware with flared rim having a distinct edge. Note broken bit end. From Black River, Jefferson County, N. Y. A. Skinner Collection, HFMAI 9/3256.

Figure 131. Trumpet pipe of red ware with flared rim. (a) Smoking chamber orifice, showing rim and bowl damage. (b) Right side, showing distinct rim edge. From Phelp's Farm site, Adams, Jefferson County, N. Y. RM 20346.

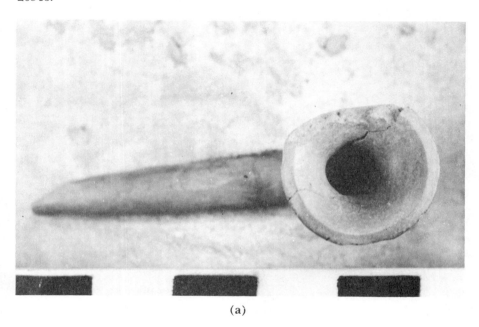

(a)

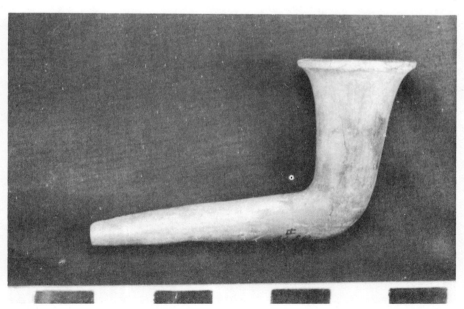

(b)

Figure 132. Trumpet pipe of tan ware with flared rim and distinct rim edge. (a) Smoking chamber orifice. (b) Right side, showing distinct bit and decoration on the remote side of the bowl: four incised grooves and a row of punctates beneath them. From Heath Farm, Rodman, Jefferson County, N. Y. RM 20349.

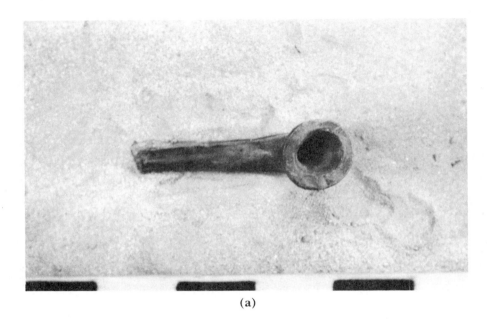

(a)

(b)

Figure 133. Trumpet pipe of tan ware with flared rim and distinct rim edge. (a) Smoking chamber orifice. (b) Right side, showing incised groove midway between rim and elbow and distinctly flared rim. From McClure-Snider site, Ontario County, N. Y. RM 18684.

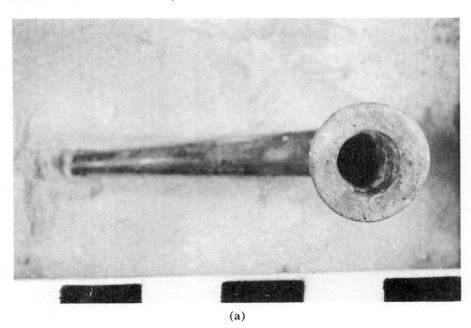

(a)

(b)

Figure 134. Trumpet pipe of tan ware having flared, distinct rim with a row of punctates encircling it. (a) Smoking chamber orifice. (b) Right side of pipe. From the Nichols site, Adams Center, Jefferson County, N. Y. RM 19481.

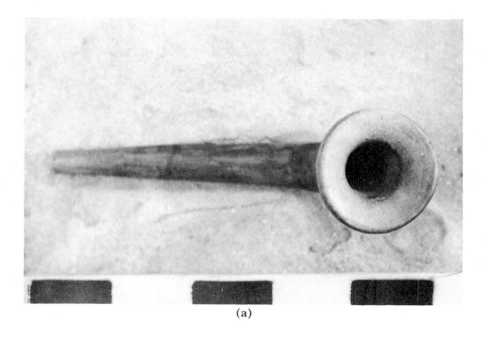

(a)

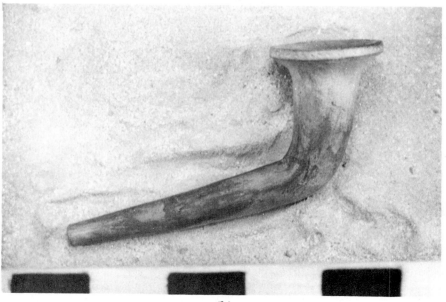

(b)

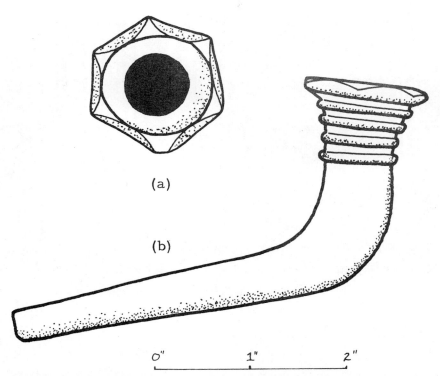

(a)

(b)

0"   1"   2"

Figure 135. Trumpet pipe of tan ware with a flared, hexagonal rim. (a) Smoking chamber orifice, showing the six-sided so-called "squash blossom" design. (b) Right side of pipe, showing the bowl decorated in the fashion of the ring-bowl pipes: the horizontal pattern of incised lines and raised rings. From the Moore site, Watertown, Jefferson County, N. Y. RM 2052.

Figure 136. **Trumpet pipe of tan ware, showing extensive decoration. The flared rim shows a row of punctates. A similar row occurs beneath the bowl design, which consists of four bands of closely incised parallel lines alternating with four wide grooves. (a) Smoking chamber orifice. (b) Right side. From the Morse Farm, Watertown, Jefferson County, N. Y. RM 20579.**

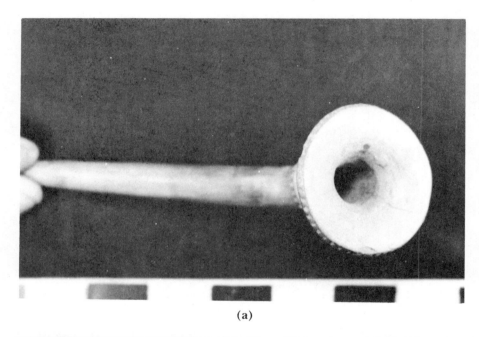

(a)

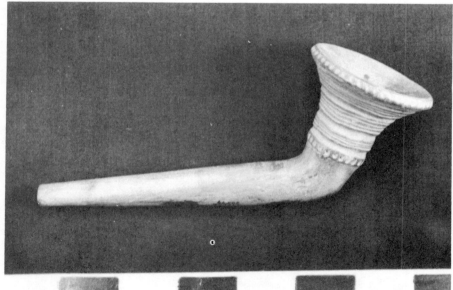

(b)

SQUARE COLLARED
(Figs. 137–140)

Physical Characteristics

The bowl of this type of pottery pipe is topped by a square-shaped rim, or collar (see Fig. 7), which is often castellated at the four corners. The lines of the bowl are generally either straight or gently flaring. Decoration usually includes horizontally incised lines on the sides of the collar with a single deep punctate at each corner. The stems are often decorated with two deep grooves extending the length of the upper stem and the near side of the bowl, dividing this surface into three rounded ridges, the outside two often decorated with punctates.

Discussion

I examined a total of 29 pipes of this style. Of these, 6 were from sites dated to the Iroquoian Culture. My sample contained 3 pipes from the Western Subarea, 4 from the Central Subarea, 7 from the Northern Subarea, and 1 from the Southern Subarea. Thirteen pipes were from sites in the Neutral area of Ontario, and 1 example originated from Huronia.

These data lead me to conclude that the square-collared obtuse-angle clay pipe is probably an Iroquoian artifact with a rather wide distribution throughout Ontario and the Northern, Central, and Western Subareas of New York State.

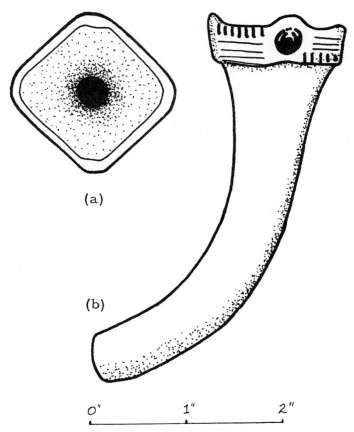

(a)

(b)

0"   1"   2"

Figure 137. Square-collared pipe of tan ware. (a) Smoking chamber orifice, showing squared rim. (b) Right side, showing design on two sides and one corner of the collar. Horizontal lines and punctates occur in all four sides of the collar in a slightly varying pattern. Large punctates appear at all four corners. From Locke, Cayuga County, N. Y. A. Skinner Collection, HFMAI 5/3828.

Figure 138. Square-collared pipe of red to brown ware. (a) Chamber orifice, showing squared rim. (b) Right side, showing side and corner designs. Each side is divided horizontally by an incised line, on either side of which occurs a row of punctates. Large, single punctates appear at each of the four corners. From Sennet township, Cayuga County, N. Y. RM 583.

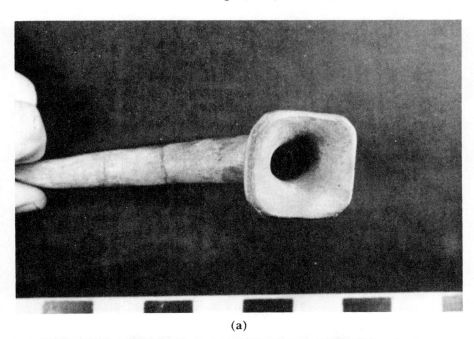

(a)

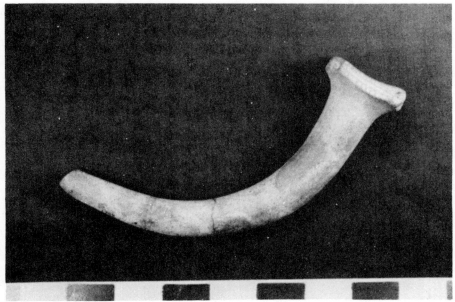

(b)

Figure 139. Square-collared pipe of tan to black ware. Distinct bit. (a) Smoking chamber orifice, showing square rim and punctates and incising on stem top. (b) Right side, showing stem and collar decoration. Two horizontal and parallel lines appear on each side of the collar, and one large punctate appears at each corner. The upper surface of the stem and the near side of the bowl carry two grooves with a row of punctates on the outer edge of each groove. From Shelby Fort, Orleans County, N. Y. RM 3006.

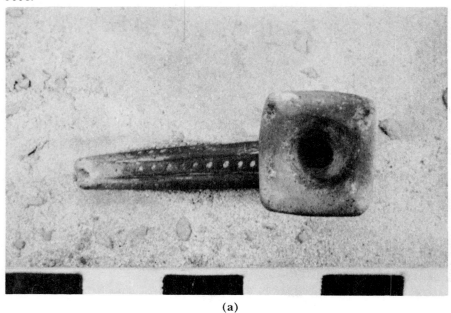

(a)

(b)

Figure 140. Square-collared pipe of tan ware, with a broken stem. (a) Smoking chamber orifice, showing squared rim and decorated stem top. (b) Right side, showing stem decoration (same as in Fig. 139) and collar markings—three horizontal and parallel grooves to each side and one large punctate at each corner. From Canoe Point, Seneca County, N. Y. RM 16.

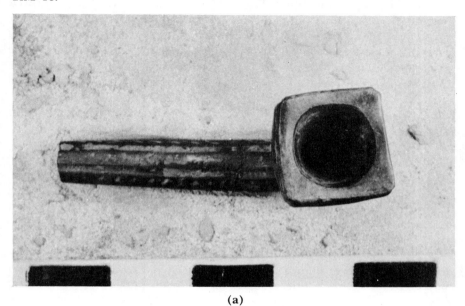

(a)

(b)

ESCUTCHEON
(Figs. 141–144)

Physical Characteristics

The left, right, and remote sides of the bowl of this type are often decorated with a horizontal pattern of incised lines, punctates, and/or rings; it is the near side of the bowl—a flattened plate or shield of clay carrying a design—that gives the pipe the name "escutcheon." The shield varies from rectangular to crescent shaped, and its decorative motifs include human effigies as well as geometrical designs. Pendergast has chosen to call the crescent-shaped escutcheon pipe a "moon" pipe (Pendergast 1966:Fig. 8, 197). The escutcheon generally rises above the rim of the rest of the bowl.

Discussion

All 13 escutcheon pipes that I examined were from sites attributed to the Iroquoian Culture and located in the Northern Subarea. Further research may result in wider archaeological and geographical distribution for this type.

Figure 141. **Crescent-shaped escutcheon pipe of red to tan ware. (a) Near side of bowl, showing human figure on the open portion of the crescent (right). (b) Right side of pipe, showing horizontal incised ring pattern on the bowl. (c) View into smoking chamber orifice, showing crescent-shaped rim formed by the escutcheon. From Jefferson County, N. Y. RM 465.**

(a)

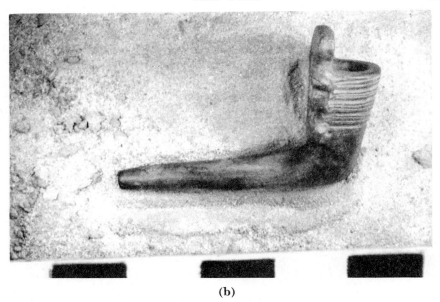

(b)

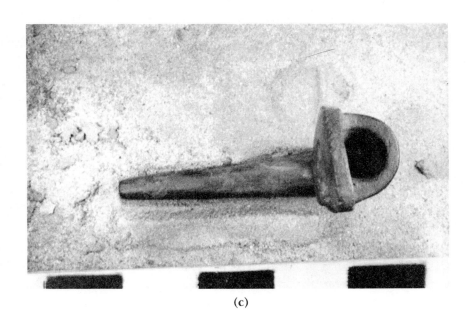

(c)

Figure 142. Crescent-shaped escutcheon pipe of dark tan ware. (a) Near side of the bowl, showing the punctate design on, and within, the crescent, which has a human effigy on its open side (right). (b) Right side of pipe, showing incised and punctate design on bowl and the human effigy under the raised escutcheon rim. (c) Smoking chamber orifice, showing the flattened side formed by the escutcheon. From the Freeman Farm, Jefferson County, N. Y. RM 20573.

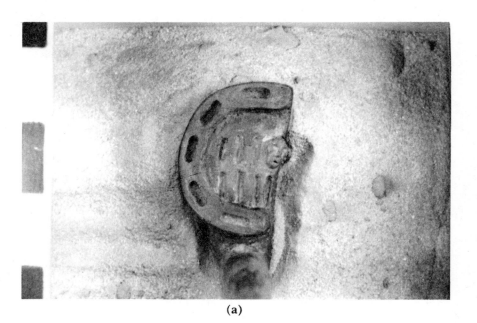

(a)

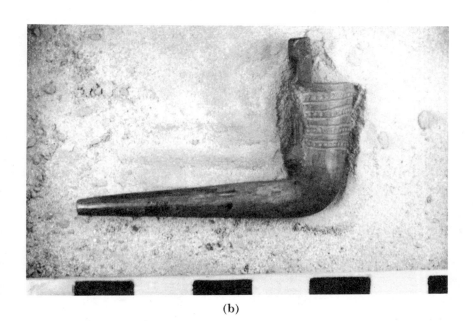

(b)

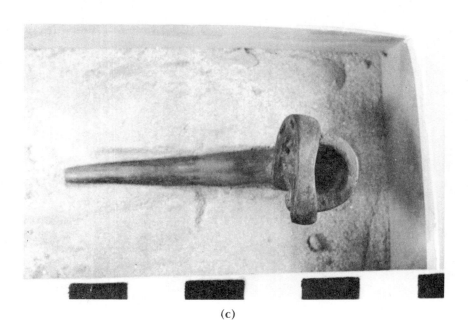

(c)

Figure 143. Escutcheon pipe of tan ware with geometrical design on the shield and the bowl. (a) Escutcheon on the near side, showing the scalloped upper edge, the punctate design at the top and the bottom, and the vertical incised design between. (b) Right side of pipe, showing horizontal incised design on the bowl. (c) Smoking chamber orifice. From the Morse Farm, Jefferson County, N. Y. RM 20574.

(a)

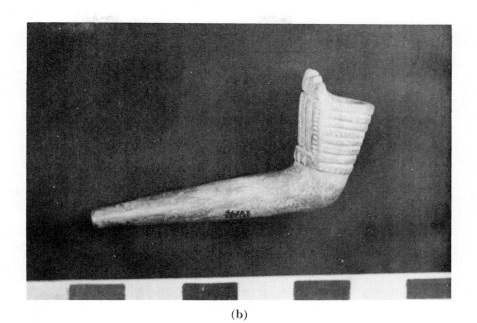

(b)

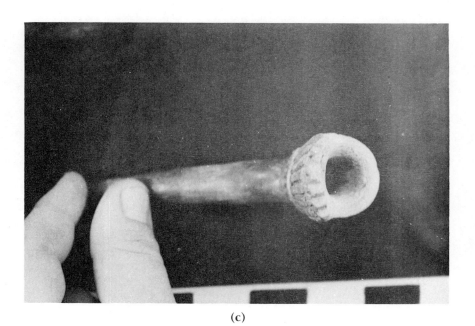

(c)

Figure 144. Escutcheon pipe of tan ware. (a) Near side, showing escutcheon with a rounded top and having a punctate and incised design. (b) **Right side of pipe, showing the horizontal pattern of incising and punctates on the bowl. (c) Smoking chamber orifice. From the Morse Farm, Jefferson County, N. Y. RM 20575.**

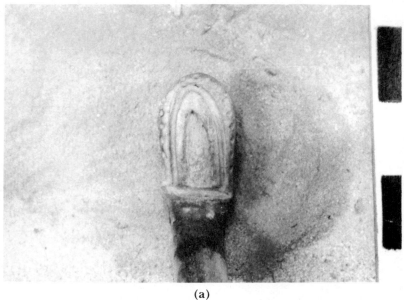

(a)

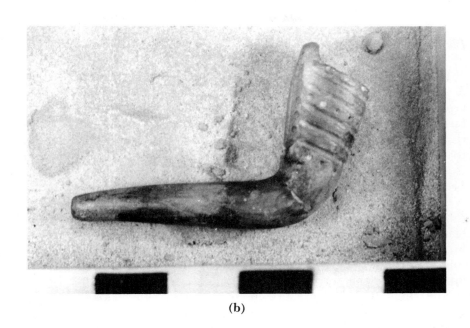

(b)

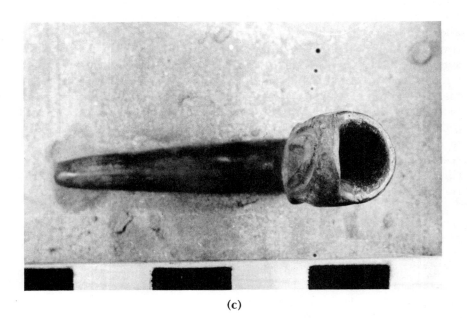

(c)

HUMAN EFFIGY
(Figs. 145–160)

Physical Characteristics

Human effigy pipes vary within the collections I have examined, as do also the theories concerning the significance of each discernible type. That there exists a great range in the ability to sculpt the human face is also apparent; some of the effigies, by modern standards of artistic and technical excellence, are extremely sophisticated. I have chosen to differentiate human effigy pipes into three groups; the designation is, however, arbitrary, and will remain so until more examples have been studied.

The first style includes those effigies that attempt to depict realistically the human face (I cannot subjectively discern any "Indianlike" features on these effigies, as do some other writers). All such "portrait" human effigy pipes share three features: the effigy appears on the near side of the bowl; a rim or collar (possibly representing a headband) appears above the forehead; horizontal incised grooves, reminiscent of the ring-bowl pipe, are present on the bowl—that is, the back of the head. The stem of the portrait variety may be decorated with rows of punctates along its length. Grooves are also often present.

The second style includes those pipes that I shall tentatively label "masklike." They differ from the portrait pipes in the following ways: no "headband" is present; the bowl has no rim collar; the mask extends above the bowl rim; the face is often slanted, with the chin pointed toward the smoker and the forehead high and pointed away from the smoker; the lateral edges of the face are separated from the bowl by a ridge depicting the side of a mask. The ears on both the portrait and masklike pipes are either rudimentary or absent (with the exception of the atypical face in Fig. 146, where they appear prominent and pierced). The masklike style usually has an undecorated stem. Study of this type and comparison with the Iroquois mask style has failed to result in any correlations; I cannot discern any characteristic or distinctive facial distortions. The bowl decoration is similar to the portrait bowl style.

The third style, and certainly the most unusual of the three, is the "distorted" human effigy pipe. The following features are characteristic of this style: the distorted cranium almost always shows signs of a headband, or at least of a horizontal incising on the forehead; the cheeks are hollow and pronounced; the cheekbones are high; the noses are aquiline. It is conjectural whether, as some suggest, these features are meant to project a man involved in a face-distorting activity, such as blowing out or sucking in. In fact, this type has often been called masklike in an attempt to draw a parallel between it and the Iroquois blowing-face mask. This analysis is open to much criticism: the faces have no mask delineation behind the jaw and ear; if they were intended to depict blowing, the cheeks would be distended and not drawn in. Indeed, I believe that the motion indicated is inhalation, perhaps of the smoke just exhaled by the smoker. Stem decoration is similar to that of the portrait style; however, the bowl decoration is a vertical, rather than a horizontal, pattern and seems to resemble that found on the bird effigy pipes (I have included a bird effigy illustration for comparison—Fig. 158). The flexed arm and leg positions are pronounced but rather stylized; they are similar to the leg shape and position on the mammal effigies (Fig. 159 is included for comparison).

I must note here that included in my statistical analysis of human effigy pipes are those examples I have already discussed: a basket-bowl pipe effigy (Fig. 103); the stem of a stone obtuse-angle pipe (Fig. 38); escutcheon pipe effigies (Figs. 141 and 142).

Discussion

Nineteen human effigy pipes were from sites identifiable by culture: 1, Owasco; 18, Iroquoian. These data may indicate that the style is a Late Woodland development. Of the total of 46 human effigies that I studied, 44 could be attributed to a given geographical area: 12, Northern Subarea; 11, Central Subarea; 1, Eastern Subarea; 18, Neutral area of Ontario; 2, Huronia, Ontario. Two examples were identified only as from New York State.

Figure 145. **Portrait style human effigy pipe of black ware. Right side of bowl (stem is broken off) shows the punctate design on the rim and the deep grooves on the right, left, and remote sides of the bowl. They end in deep punctates behind the face. From the W. G. Raine's Farm, Ontario County, N. Y. HFMAI 4/1122.**

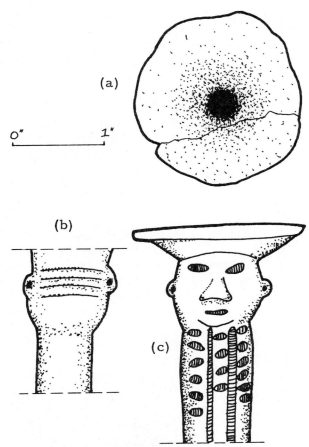

Figure 146. Portrait style human effigy pipe of black to tan ware. (a) Smoking chamber orifice, showing wide rim (damaged). (b) View of remote side of bowl only, showing four horizontal and parallel incised lines ending behind the prominent ears, which are pierced through. (c) View of the near side, showing effigy, wide rim, pierced ears, and the grooved and punctate design typical of the stem and lower bowl regions of most portrait human effigy pipes. Stem is not shown. From Scipioville, Cayuga County, N. Y. HFMAI 9/4502.

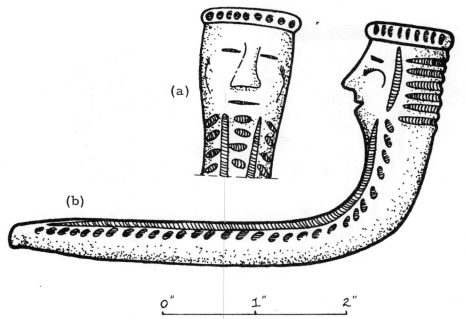

Figure 147. Portrait style human effigy pipe of tan to black ware. (a) View of near side, showing effigy, rudimentary ears, punctate rim, and grooved and punctate stem. (b) Right side, showing horizontal groove and ring pattern on the bowl and the groove and punctate pattern on the stem. From the L. Desmann Farm, Monroe County, N. Y. Collection of Newton Farwell, Geneva, N. Y.

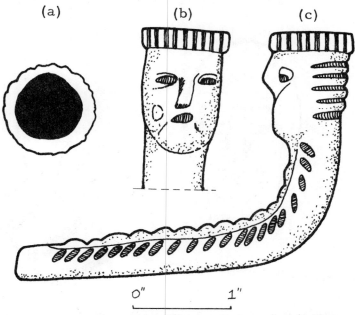

Figure 148. Portrait style human effigy pipe of gray ware. (a) Smoking chamber orifice. (b) View of near side of the bowl, showing the effigy and the rim design of vertical incising. (c) Right side, showing horizontal incising and the ring pattern on the bowl and the groove and punctate pattern on the stem. From the Boughton Hill site, Ontario County, N. Y. H. L. Schoff Collection. HFMAI 22/3298.

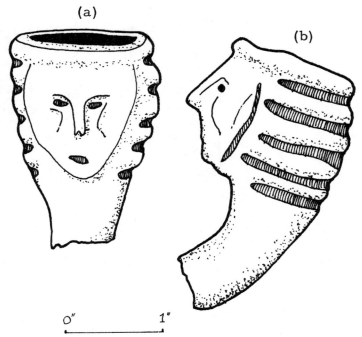

(a)

(b)

Figure 149. Masklike human effigy pipe of dark gray ware. (a) View of near side, showing effigy. (b) Right side, showing horizontal and ring pattern of the bowl decoration and the sloping of the "mask." Note the ridge behind the high cheekbones, which may represent the edge of the mask. The rim on the near side is higher than the rim on the lateral and remote sides of the bowl. The stem has been broken. From the Hopewell site, Ontario County, N. Y. Collection of Newton Farwell, Geneva, N. Y.

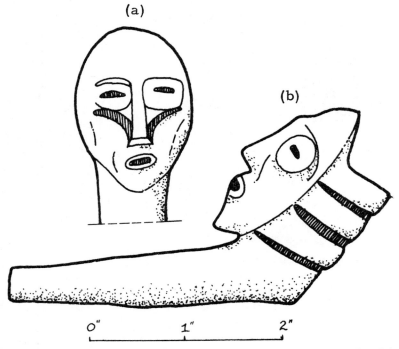

(a)

(b)

Figure 150. Masklike human effigy pipe of tan ware. (a) Near side of bowl showing oval, masklike effigy. (b) Right side of pipe, showing horizontal incising and ring pattern on the lateral and remote sides of the bowl. From the E. D. Hlec Farm, N. Y. Terry Collection, American Museum of Natural History, No. 2725.

Figure 151. Masklike human effigy pipe of brown to tan ware. (a) Near side, showing effigy. (b) Right side of pipe, showing mask and high rim in the mask section. Horizontal incising and rings form the pattern on the remote and lateral sides of the bowl. A hole is present behind the mask. (c) Smoking chamber orifice. From the Morse Farm, Jefferson County, N. Y. RM 594.

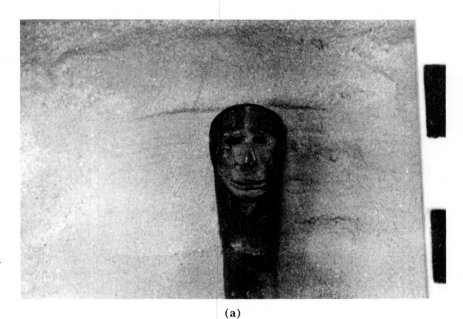

(a)

(b)

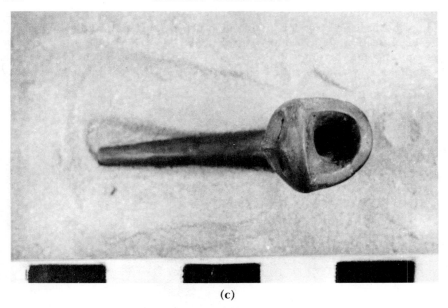

(c)

Figure 152. Masklike human effigy pipe of tan to brown ware. (a) Near side showing effigy. (b) Right side of pipe, showing side of effigy and the horizontal, ring, and punctate pattern on the remainder of the bowl. Rudimentary "ears" are present as holes. (c) Smoking chamber orifice. From the Talcott Farm, Jefferson County, N. Y. RM 20572.

(a)

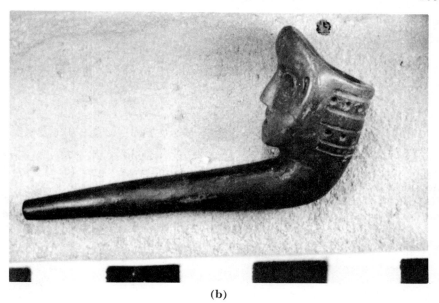

(b)

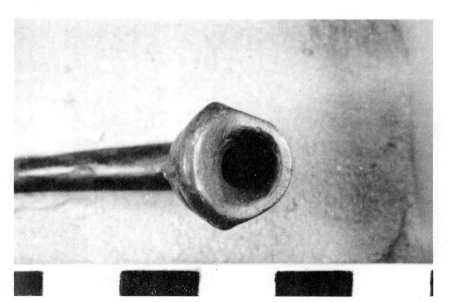

(c)

Figure 153. Masklike human effigy pipe of tan ware. (a) View of punctate design on the remote side of the bowl and under the rim. (b) View of the smoking chamber orifice, which forms the mouth of the effigy. (c) View of the right side of the pipe, showing the effigy facing upward, in the usual smoking chamber orifice position, leaving the near side of the bowl proper undecorated. From the Ellisburg site, Jefferson County, N. Y. RM 3002.

(a)

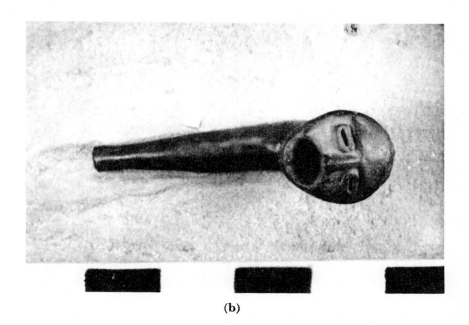

(b)

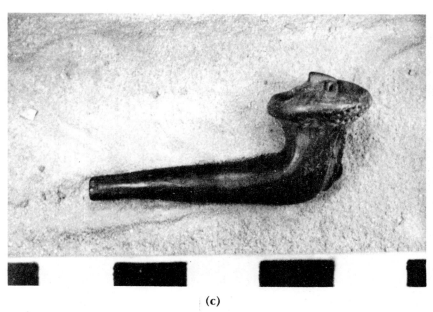

(c)

Figure 154. Masklike human effigy pipe of tan ware. (a) View of the near side of the bowl with effigy. (b) Right side of pipe, which is undecorated except for the effigy. From the Calligan Farm, Jefferson County, N. Y. RM 20578.

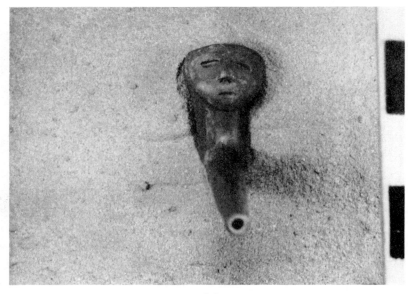

(a)

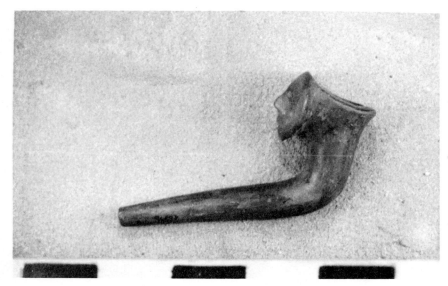

(b)

Figure 155. Masklike human effigy pipe of tan ware. (a) Near side of the bowl, showing the effigy. (The "earlike" projections are actually the rings on the bowl protruding from behind the mask.) (b) Right side of pipe, showing the horizontal incising and ring pattern on the lateral and remote sides of the bowl. From the Heath Farm, Jefferson County, N. Y. RM 597.

(a)

(b)

Figure 156. Distorted human effigy pipe of tan to red ware. (a) Smoking chamber orifice, showing effigy head projecting from the near side of the bowl. (b) Right side of the pipe, showing the effigy body forming the rim, with its head projecting toward the smoker on the near side. Note the vertical incising on the rim-body, the incised "headband" on the effigy forehead, and the position of the arms and legs. One ridge extends on the right and left sides from beneath the rim to just below the elbow. From the Dann site, Monroe County, N. Y. RM 37829.

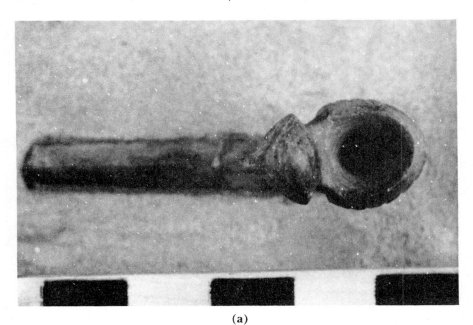

(a)

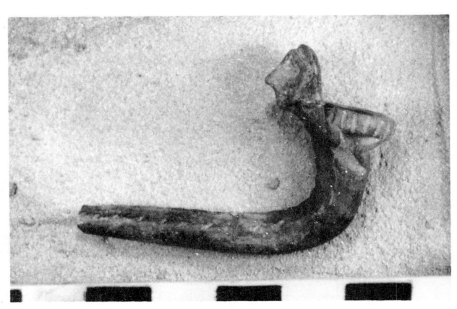

(b)

Figure 157. Distorted human effigy pipe of black ware. (a) **Right side,** showing stem decorated with two lateral rows of punctates extending its length and up the bowl almost to the rim. As in Fig. 156, the rim is formed by the effigy's body and carries vertical incising. (b) **The head of** the effigy faces the smoker. (c) Smoking chamber orifice. From the Dann site, Monroe County, N. Y. RM 37828.

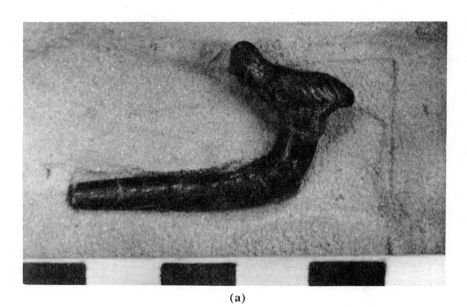

(a)

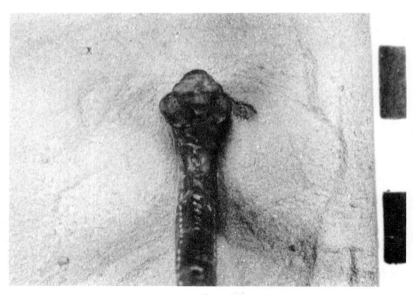

(b)

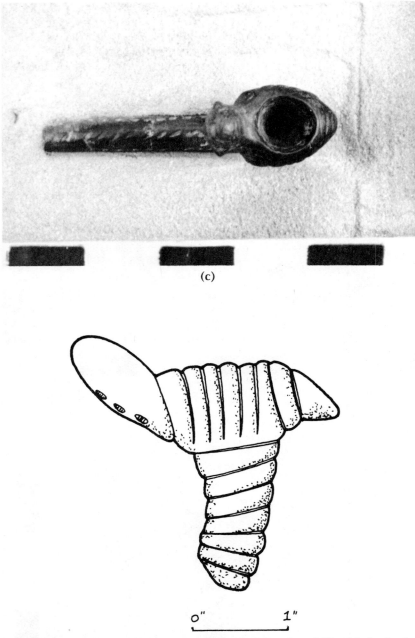

(c)

0"   1"

Figure 158. Animal effigy of tan ware, probably a hawklike bird; the head is missing. The pipe is included here for comparison with Figs. 156 and 157, which show somewhat similar decoration. It is obviously very difficult to determine what may be a distorted human effigy from what may be an animal effigy. From Cayuga Lake, Cayuga County, N. Y. HFMAI 22/3766.

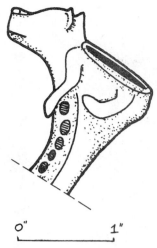

0"   1"

Figure 159. Right side of bowl area only of mammal effigy pipe constructed of dark tan ware (for entire pipe, see Fig. 167). Compare the positions of the legs with the arm and leg positions on Figs. 156 and 157. From the Boughton Hill site, Ontario County, N. Y. Collection of Newton Farwell, Geneva, N. Y.

Figure 160. Distorted human effigy pipe of black ware. (a) **Smoking chamber orifice, showing bulging effigy area on near side of bowl. (b) Right side of pipe, showing the raised head of the effigy on the near side of the bowl and a general body image on the rim. The legs and arms are in positions similar to those of Figs. 156 and 157. Some incised and punctate decoration appears laterally. All features are sufficiently vague so as to make the human characteristics moot. From the Warren site, Ontario County, N. Y. RM 3009.**

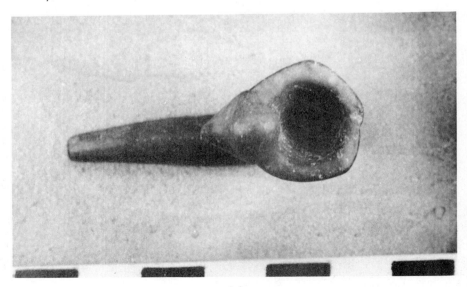

(a)

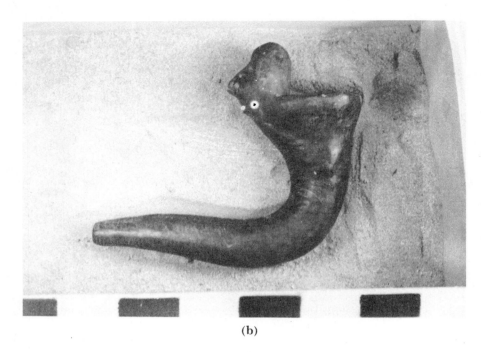

(b)

MAMMAL EFFIGY
(Figs. 161–167)

Physical Characteristics

This style of pipe may be described as an obtuse-angle effigy pipe in which the animal's body often forms the rim of the pipe, with its head projecting toward the smoker from the near side of the bowl and its tail, if present, extending from the remote side. The legs usually occupy positions similar to those of the arms and legs of the distorted human effigy pipes. As I have already mentioned, it is often very difficult to differentiate between the distorted human effigy pipe and the mammal effigy pipe. I have applied the general term "mammal" to this type, often referred to in the literature as "wolf" or "bear" effigy pipes, because of the extreme subjectivity involved in deciding which is bear, which wolf, which dog, and, indeed, which human.

Discussion

Like most of the other effigy pipes, the mammal effigy pipes are apparently Iroquoian artifacts. Of eight pipes identifiable by culture, all were Iroquoian. Of the 27 examples with geographical provenience, 10 were from the Central Subarea, 2 were from the Western Subarea, and 1 each was from the Northern, Eastern, and Southern Subareas. Ten were from the Neutral area of Ontario, and 1 pipe was identified only as originating in New York State.

Figure 161. Mammal effigy pipe of tan ware, undecorated except for the head on the near side of the bowl. (a) Smoking chamber orifice, showing effigy. (b) Right side. From Heath Farm, Jefferson County, N.Y. RM 20397.

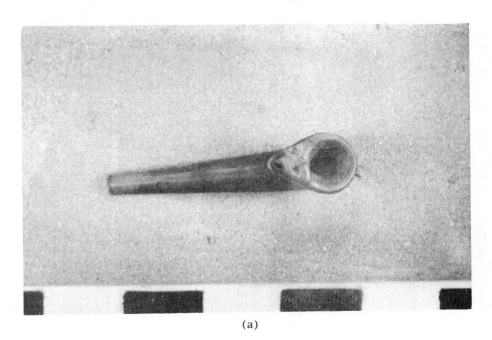

(a)

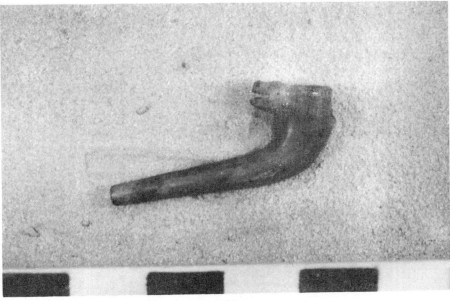

(b)

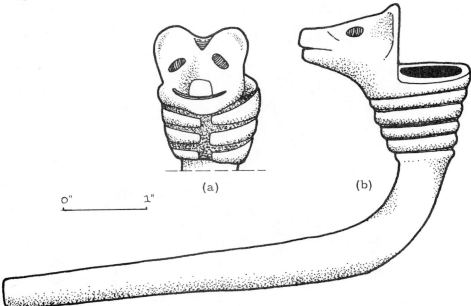

(a)   (b)

0"_____1"

Figure 162. Mammal effigy of black ware. (a) Near side of bowl, showing effigy head; the grooves circumventing the bowl end under the effigy's chin. (b) Right side, showing the effigy profile and the horizontal incising and ring pattern of the bowl. The stem is undecorated. From Cayuga Lake, Seneca or Cayuga County, N. Y. HFMAI 22/3765.

Figure 163. Probable mammal effigy of tan ware with broken stem. (a) Chamber orifice, showing effigy facing the smoker on the near side of the bowl. (b) Right side, showing the raised rim over the head of the effigy and the horizontal incising and ring pattern on the bowl. (c) Right side, showing the raised parts of the rim that may represent the animal's ears. From the Cattaraugus Reservation, Cattaraugus County, N. Y. HFMAI 10/3673.

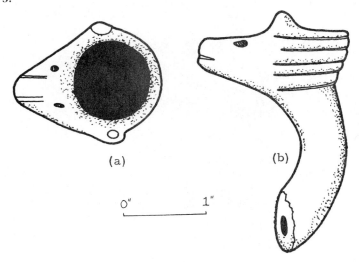

(a)   (b)

0"_____1"

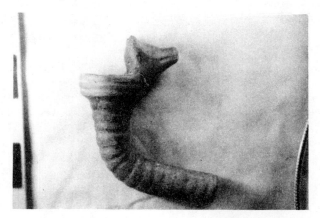

Figure 164. Mammal effigy of tan ware, with a broken stem. Left side of pipe shows the effigy with prominent features and ringed bowl and stem design. Effigy is on near side of bowl. From the **Dann site, Monroe County, N. Y. H. L.** Schoff Collection, HFMAI 22/2952.

Figure 165. Mammal effigy of tan ware. Right side of the pipe shows the effigy with prominent features and a bulbar bowl, possibly suggesting the body of the animal. The two top horizontal incised lines on the bowl extend along the animal's "neck." One row of punctates appears beneath the bowl. From the Dann site, Monroe County, N. Y. H. L. Schoff Collection, HFMAI 22/2951.

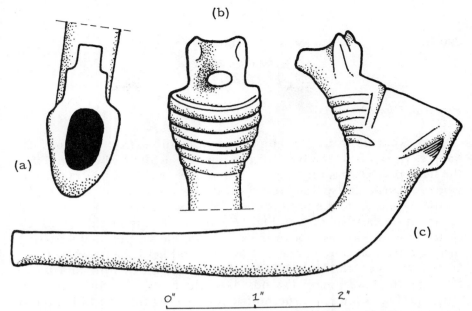

Figure 166. Mammal effigy of black ware. (a) Smoking chamber orifice. (b) Near side of the bowl, showing the effigy head. The bowl beneath the head is decorated with horizontal incising and rings, while the remainder of the bowl is undecorated. (c) Right side of the pipe, showing the effigy with prominent features, including nose area, ears, and front and back legs. From the Boughton Hill site, Ontario County, N. Y. Collection of Newton Farwell, Geneva, N. Y.

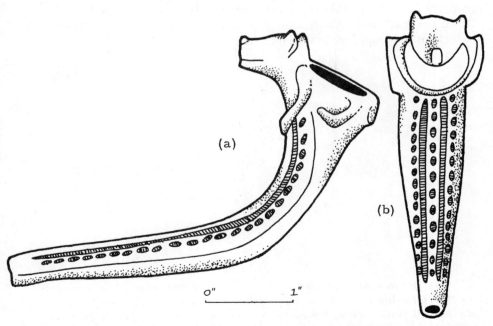

Figure 167. Probable mammal effigy of dark tan ware (shown partially, for comparison, as Fig. 159). (a) Right side of pipe, showing definite features of ears, nose, mouth, and front and back legs. A lateral ridge appears beneath the punctates. (b) View of the stem top and the near side of the bowl. The three rows of punctates are separated by two deep grooves running the length of the stem. From the Boughton Hill site, Ontario County, N. Y. Collection of Newton Farwell, Geneva, N. Y.

BIRD EFFIGY
(Figs. 168–174)

Physical Characteristics

Two types of bird effigy pipes are discernible from my research sample. In the first, the bowl of the pipe forms the body of the bird, the head projects from the near side and may or may not be characteristic of a particular species, and the tail projects from the remote side. In the second, only the head of the bird appears, and it may be found either on the near side (as in Fig. 173) or on the remote side, in which case it faces upward as though the stem were the long neck of a wading bird, a resemblance reinforced by the bill and head shapes (Fig. 172). In the first type, the body is often decorated with incising and punctates and the head usually extends above the bowl's rim. In the second type, the bill is long and the nostrils are prominent; the bill extends far above the bowl rim.

Discussion

Again, the bird effigy pipe is apparently an Iroquoian artifact; all 9 examples from identifiable sites were attributed to this culture. The geographical distribution of my sample is wide: 4 each from the Central and Northern Subareas and from the Neutral area of Ontario; 3 from the Eastern Subarea; and 2 from the Western Subarea. One pipe was identified only as New York State.

Note: *Because of a scarcity of specimens that are intact, I have included in the following illustrations what appear to be effigies broken from pipes. In partial justification, I must state that unlike other types of effigies—for example, human and mammal—the bird effigy in clay does not seem to be found on Iroquoian artifacts other than pipes.*

Figure 168. Bird effigy of tan ware with broken stem. (a) Left side, showing tail on remote side and head on near side, with definite eye and mouth, punctate design on the throat, vertical incising on the body-rim-bowl area, and horizontal incising on the remaining part of the stem. (b) Smoking chamber orifice, showing the head and tail protrusions and the deep incising around the rim extending from the orifice. (c) Near side of bowl, showing effigy. From the Dann site, Monroe County, N. Y. RM 18425.

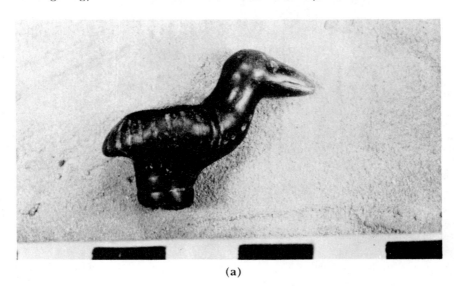

(a)

(b)

(c)

Figure 169. Bird effigy of tan ware with broken stem and damaged bowl. (a) Left side, showing head extending from the near side of the bowl. The eye and mouth are prominent, and the tail extends from the remote side of the bowl. The body (bowl) is marked with diagonal incising, suggesting, perhaps, the pattern of wings. (b) Smoking chamber orifice, showing damaged right side. The rim incising is probably similar to that shown in Fig. 168b. (c) Near side of bowl, showing effigy. From Chimney Island, Jefferson County, N. Y. RM 20400.

(a)

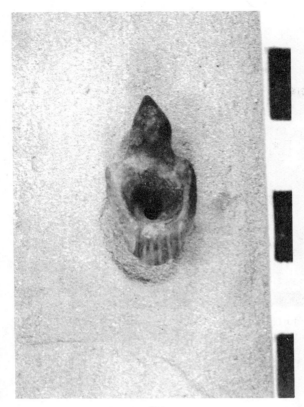

(b)

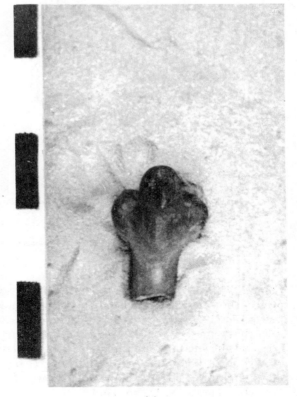

(c)

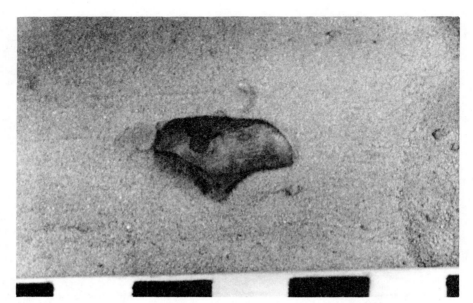

Figure 170. Head of a predatorlike bird, tan ware, possibly broken from a pipe. Four horizontal lines appear on each side of the beak and the eyes and nostrils are formed by deep punctates. From the Nichols Pond site, Madison County, N. Y. RM 19327.

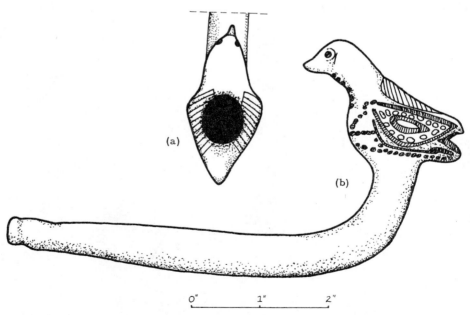

(a)

(b)

0"   1"   2"

Figure 171. Bird effigy pipe of dark brown ware. (a) Smoking chamber orifice, showing the effigy head facing the smoker on the near side of the bowl. Closely spaced, diagonally slanted, incised lines appear on either side above the wings. (b) Right side, showing the pronounced punctate eyes and the incising and punctate design intended to emphasize the shape of the bird's body and wings. The tail is sculpted and decorated. From the Boughton Hill site, Ontario County, N. Y. Collection of Newton Farwell, Geneva, N. Y. No. 1744.

Figure 172. Bird effigy of tan ware. (a) View of right side. (b) Remote side of the bowl, showing the effigy with punctate eyes (at bowl bottom, near the heel) and nostrils. The near side of the bowl resembles a basket-bowl pipe, with a bulging bowl decorated with punctates and horizontal incising. The bill, probably of a wading bird, extends well above the rim and shows a distinct mouth and vertical incising in the area where the bill joins the head. (c) Smoking chamber orifice. (d) Near side of bowl. From Scipioville, Cayuga County, N. Y. American Museum of Natural History, No. 501.

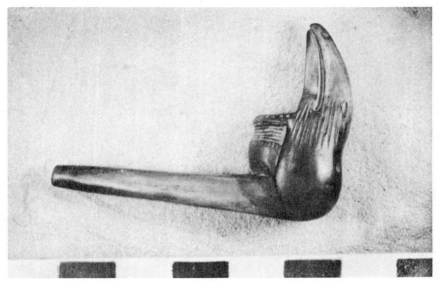

(a)

(b)

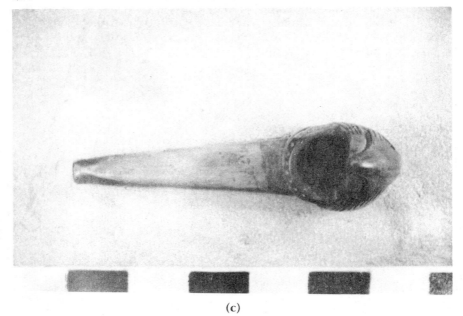

(c)

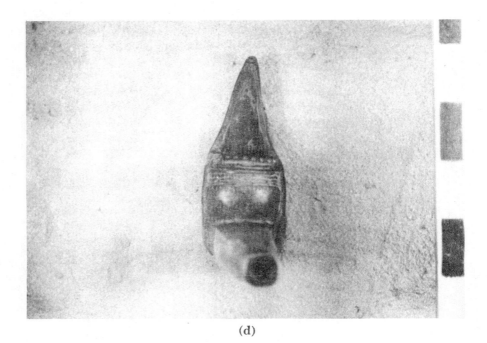

(d)

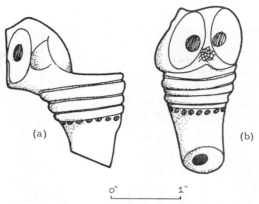

Figure 173. Owl effigy of black ware, showing ear and beak damage. (a) View of right side (assumed by the curvature of the remaining broken stem), showing effigy raised above the rim of the bowl. The horizontal groove and ring pattern circles the entire bowl, and a row of punctates appears beneath the lowest ring. (b) View of near side of bowl, showing the effigy. Deep punctates form the eyes, which are set in shallow depressions. From the Cattaraugus Reservation, Cattaraugus County, N. Y. W. L. Bryant Collection, HFMAI 10/3666.

Figure 174. Owl effigies that may well be fragments broken from pipe bowls. All are of tan ware and are decorated with geometrical groupings of punctates and incisings to give the impression of the owl—deep and large eyes, prominent beak, and peaked ears. From the Nichols Pond site, Madison County, N. Y. (a) RM 19324. (b) RM 19323. (c) RM 592.

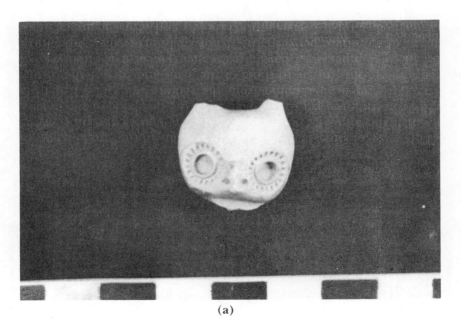

(a)

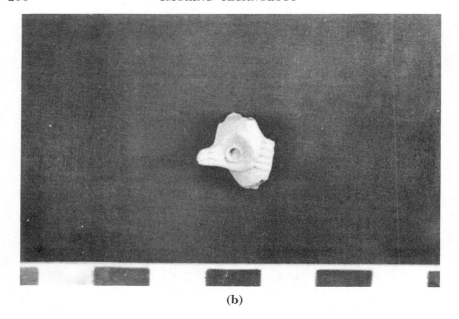

(b)

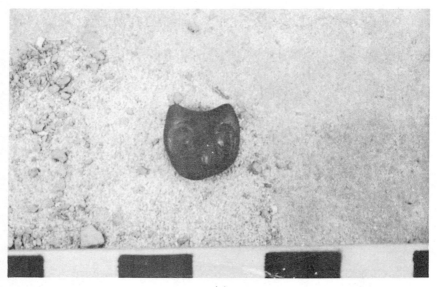

(c)

OPEN-MOUTH EFFIGY
(Figs. 175–176)

Physical Characteristics

Although to some researchers these effigy pipes may represent hungry young birds, I think such a classification is too arbitrary; this type may suggest other animals as well, for example, reptiles. I have therefore chosen the term "open-mouth" because all examples shared this bowl characteristic. The open jaw forms the rim of the bowl and the effigy may face either toward or away from the smoker. The latter position is the more atypical of pipes from the Iroquoian Culture.

Discussion

The open-mouth effigy pipe was represented in my sample by 5 artifacts from sites attributed to the Iroquoian Culture. Eight examples had known provenience: 2 each from the Western and Northern Subareas; 1, Central Subarea; 2, Neutral area of Ontario. One pipe was attributed only to New York State.

Figure 175. Open-mouth effigy pipe of dark tan to brown ware. (a) **Near side of the bowl, showing the top of the animal's head with punctates forming its eyes. (b) Right side of the pipe, showing the effigy profile and the stem design: lightly incised cross hatching on the stem top and incised grooves forming rings parallel to the bit end on the stem bottom. (c) Smoking chamber orifice, formed by the open jaws of the animal. From the Morse Farm, Jefferson County, N. Y. RM 20398.**

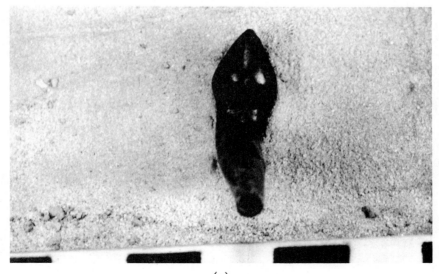

(a)

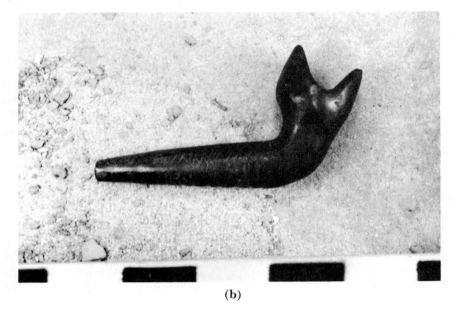

(b)

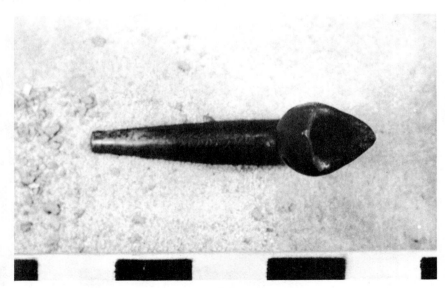

(c)

Figure 176. Open-mouth effigy pipe of black ware, partially restored. (a) View of near side of bowl. (b) Right side of the pipe, showing the effigy facing the smoker—that is, the head and punctate eyes are located on the remote side of the bowl. Undecorated other than the effigy. From the Buffam Street site, Erie County. RM 17632.

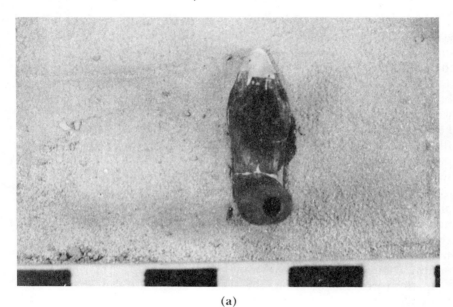

(a)

(b)

REPTILE AND AMPHIBIAN EFFIGY
(Figs. 177–183)

Physical Characteristics

For purposes of description, the reptile and amphibian effigy category may be broken down into three main types: the twining snake; the salamander; and the turtle. The twining snake effigy represents that reptile as a ridge twined about the bowl and stem of the pipe. The snake's head is usually found on the near side of the bowl just below the rim, forming one end of the coil. Several pipes I examined were like the twining snake pipe with the exception that no reptile head or tail was present; I have included one such pipe among my illustrations, although I have not included it in my statistics. It is present purely for comparison and to point out once again the difficulty in differentiating similar artifacts into distinct groups (see Fig. 179).

The second classification has been called both the salamander pipe and the lizard pipe. I prefer the former name because these animals are more common in the New York area and are thus more probably the animals depicted. The salamander is usually found grasping the bowl with all four legs, his head under or above the rim and his tail ending somewhere on the stem past the elbow.

In the third classification, the turtle's effigy is found affixed to the bowl with the shell on either the remote or the near side of the bowl.

Discussion

The three examples that I studied which were identifiable by culture were all Iroquoian. Eight pipes were attributed to sites from cultural areas: 3, Northern Subarea; 1 each, Western and Central Subareas; 3, Neutral area of Ontario. An additional two were identified only as New York State artifacts.

Figure 177. Twining snake effigy of tan ware. (a) View into smoking chamber orifice. (b) Right side, showing the head of the snake just under the rim on the near side of the bowl. The tail is represented by a bulge just before the bit on the bottom of the stem. (c) Near side of bowl. From the Warren site, Ontario County, N. Y. RM 18308.

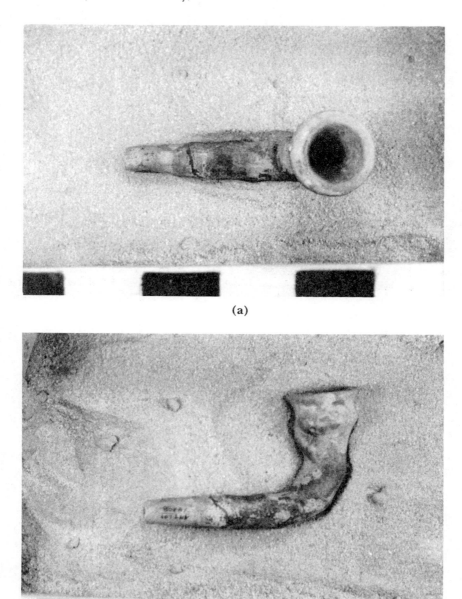

(a)

(b)

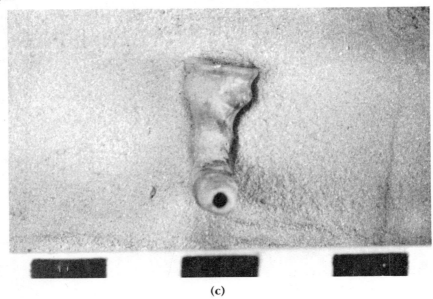

(c)

Figure 178. Twining snake effigy of dark tan ware. (a) View into smoking chamber orifice. (b) Near side of bowl, showing snake's head (with punctate eyes) toward the right. The tail is at the bit end. (c) Right side. From the Silverheels site, Erie County, N. Y. RM 20582.

(a)

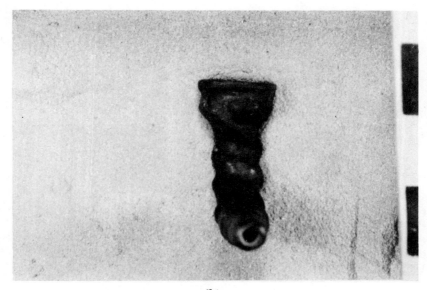

(b)

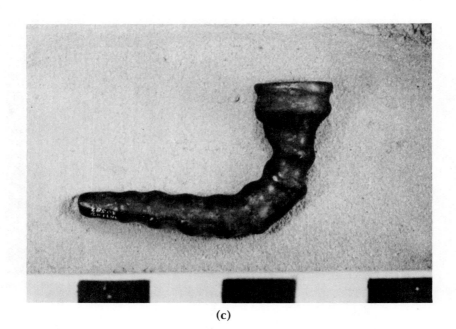

(c)

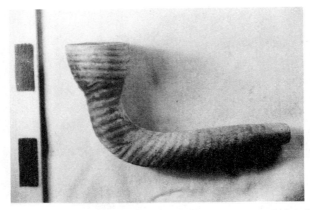

Figure 179. Obtuse-angle pipe with spiral raised coil completely encircling the bowl and the stem. It is included here because of its resemblance to the twining snake effigy. It is constructed of tan to brownish red ware. From the Gus Warren site, Ontario County, N. Y. H. L. Schoff Collection, HFMAI 22/3499.

Figure 180. Salamander pipe of tan ware. (a) Right side, showing salamander. (b) View of top of stem and the near side of the bowl. One salamander appears on each side of the bowl. (c) View into smoking chamber orifice. Note that the heads are joined around the rim by a band of clay. The heads with punctate eyes extend above the rim and the legs appear to grasp the bowl securely. Heath Farm, Jefferson County, N. Y. RM 2096.

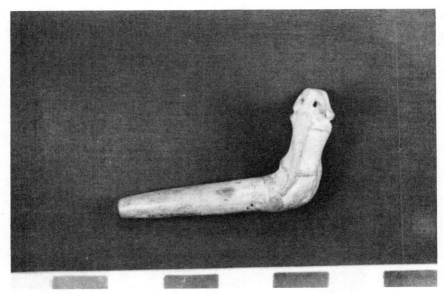

(a)

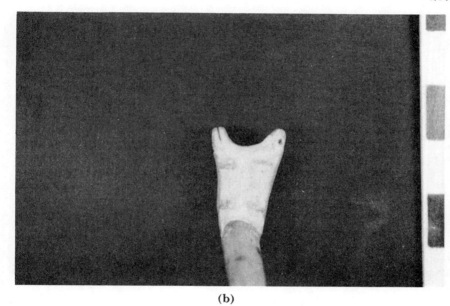

(b)

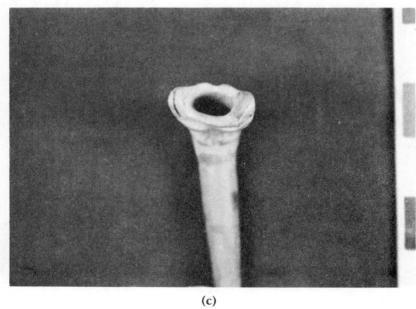

(c)

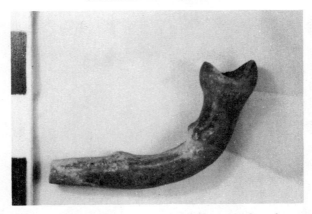

Figure 181. Probable double salamander effigy, with salamanders on the near and remote sides of the bowl. Right side of black ware pipe shows probable heads extending above the rim. Punctate marks appear on the stem, especially along the top. The details are very vague. From the Boughton Hill site, Ontario County, N. Y. H. L. Schoff Collection, HFMAI 22/3308.

Figure 182. Turtle effigy pipe of dark brown to black ware, with the effigy on the near side. (a) The near side of bowl, showing the head of the turtle near the rim, the legs grasping the bowl, and the tail extending toward the stem at the bowl bottom. (b) Right side, showing distinct rim high at the effigy side. (c) Smoking chamber orifice. From Jefferson County, N. Y. RM 20403.

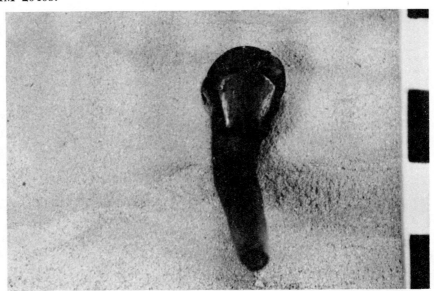

(a)

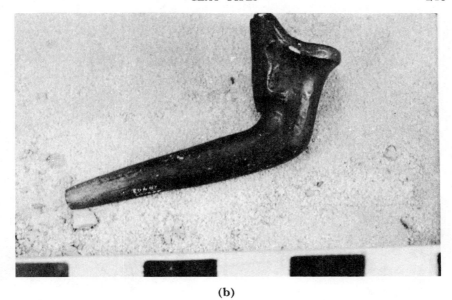

(b)

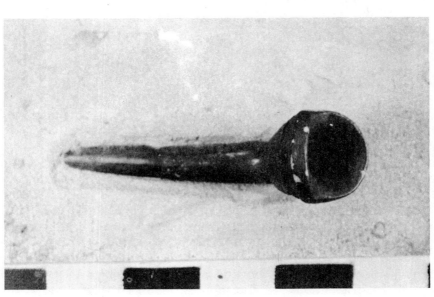

(c)

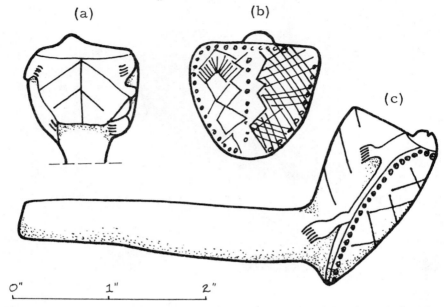

(a)   (b)

(c)

0"   1"   2"

Figure 183. **Turtle effigy of tan ware. (a) Near side of bowl, with incising indicating that it is meant to be the underside of the turtle's body. (b) Detail of the remote side of the bowl, intended to represent the turtle's shell and partly extended head. Note the punctate and incised geometrical pattern. (c) Right side of the pipe, showing the legs grasping the lateral bowl. New York State is the only provenience. Seen in unidentified collection at the Cayuga Museum, Auburn, N. Y.**

MISCELLANEOUS OBTUSE ANGLE
(Figs. 184–191)

Physical Characteristics

I have termed "miscellaneous" those pipes which do not meet my arbitrary specifications for the previously defined types. It seemed safer to me to place indefinite examples or possible variations of a given type into such a "misfit" category so that the student could decide for himself the position these artifacts occupy in the archaeology of the area.

The first example, Fig. 184, has a squared bowl and a castellated rim; it may have been modeled after the distinctive castellated ceramic pot of the Iroquois (Ritchie 1965:320). It is included with the miscellaneous examples and not with the square-collared pipes because of the atypical bowl shape, showing a geometrical bulge in its central portion. Its castellations are also more pronounced than those of the square-collared pipes.

The two pipes in Figs. 185 and 186 have flattened sides with mortice-like depressions set into one or more sides on or below the rim. In the case in which the depressions face the smoker—that is, are on the near side—the pipe may possibly indicate itself to be a relative of the escutcheon style.

The pipes in Figs. 187–189 and 191 may correctly be called a type or subtype because of their diminutive size rather than any bowl characteristics. The term "pipette" was used in the catalogue of the State Museum at Albany to describe pipes of this very small size. Figures 187 and 188 illustrate pipette pipes of similar construction: obtuse angle; gently flaring rim; and undecorated or lightly incised. Figures 189 and 191 are rather triangular in shape and are decorated with incising and punctates in a sort of "crazy-quilt" geometrical pattern. Figure 190 resembles Figs. 189 and 191 remarkably, although it is much larger. All three pipes originate from the same site, and thus may represent a local tradition, other examples of which may be found later in existing collections or in still unexcavated sites.

Discussion

Statistics for such a general category are fairly meaningless, except that they may show the proportion of these untyped pipes in my research. The 31 miscellaneous pipes attributable to sites of a given culture are all Iroquoian. The geographical distribution is very wide: 6, Western Subarea; 18 each, Central and Northern Subareas; 2 each, Eastern and Southern Subareas. Thirty-one pipes were from New York State but not attributed to a specific subcultural area; no examples were attributed to Canadian sites.

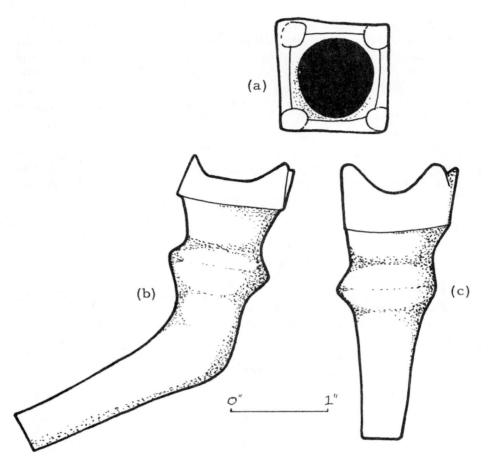

Figure 184. Obtuse-angle pipe of tan ware with geometrical bulge in the bowl. (a) Smoking chamber orifice, showing square rim. (b) Right side, showing castellated collar. (c) The near side of the bowl and the top of the stem. From Watertown, Jefferson County, N. Y. Terry Collection, Natural History Museum, No. 2720T.

Figure 185. Obtuse-angle pipe of gray ware with squared-off flattened sides. Rectangular depressions appear on the lateral and remote sides of the rim. (a) Smoking material chamber orifice, showing lateral rim depressions. (b) Right side, tilted slightly to illustrate the flattened sides and lateral depressions. (c) Remote side of bowl with depressions. From Wadsworth Gravel Pit, Fall Brook, Livingston County, N. Y. RM 34432.

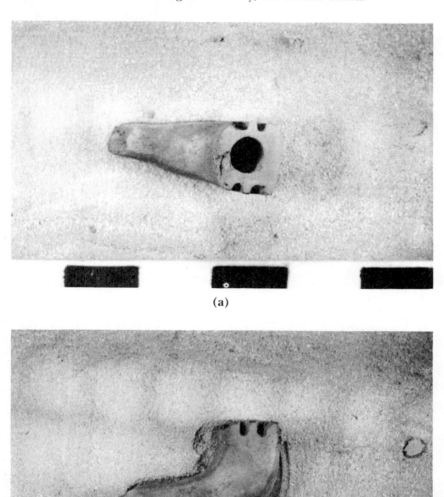

(a)

(b)

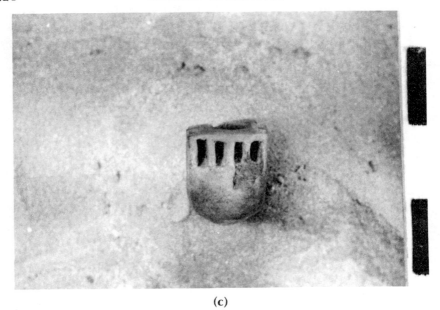

(c)

Figure 186. Obtuse-angle pipe of gray to brown ware. View is from above, showing incised grooves on the near side of the bowl and the smoking chamber and stem bore orifices. Note restoration. From the Nichols site, Jefferson County, N. Y. RM 19480.

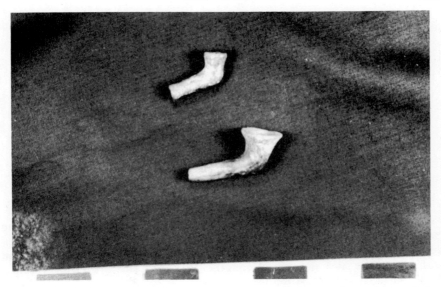

Figure 187. (a) Pipette obtuse-angle pipe of tan ware. Right side shows slightly flared rim and bit definition. From the Moore site, Jefferson County, N. Y. RM 20358. (b) Pipette obtuse-angle pipe of tan ware with flared rim, decorated by light, diagonal incising. From the Heath Farm, Jefferson County, N. Y. RM 20356.

(a)   (b)

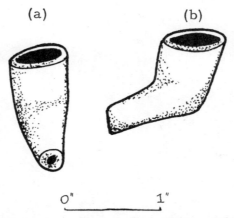

0"   1"

Figure 188. Pipette obtuse-angle pipe of tan ware, undecorated. (a) Near side of the bowl and the top of the stem, showing the bit end with the stem-bore orifice. (b) Right side, slightly tilted to show the rim and the smoking chamber orifice. From the Jack's Reef site, Onondaga County, N. Y. Collection of W. E. Perkins, Fulton, N. Y.

(a)   (b)

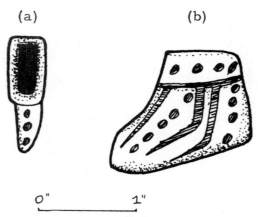

0"   1"

Figure 189. Pipette obtuse-angle pipe, triangular in shape. (a) Smoking chamber orifice and the top of the stem, showing the stem's punctate design and the narrowness of the pipe. (b) Right side, showing the decorated rim with punctates and incising. From the Ellisburg site, Jefferson County, N. Y. New York State Museum at Albany, No. 20402.

Figure 190. (a) Right side of triangular pipe of tan ware with a short, thin, protruding stem. Decorated with a geometrical "crazy-quilt" pattern. The general shape is similar to the pipette pipes in Figs. 189 and 191, but this example is larger. (b) Smoking chamber orifice. From the Ellisburg site, Jefferson County, N. Y. RM 19381.

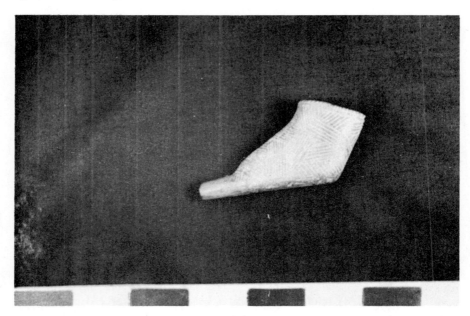

(a)

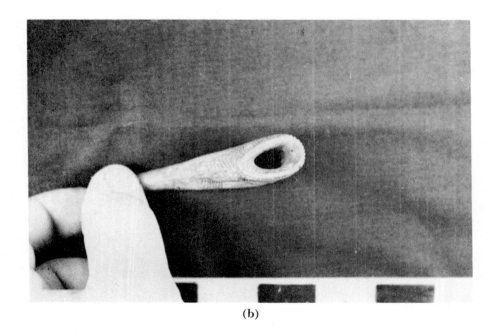

(b)

Figure 191. Pipette obtuse-angle pipe of tan ware. (a) Remote side of the bowl, showing the incised "V" design. Vertical incising encircles the rim, under which appears one deep horizontal groove. (b) Right side of the pipe, showing punctate and incised line design. From the Ellisburg site, Jefferson County, N. Y. RM 19383.

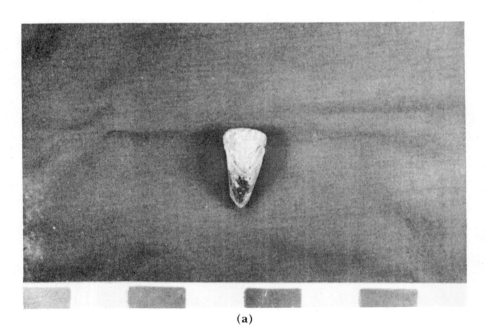

(a)

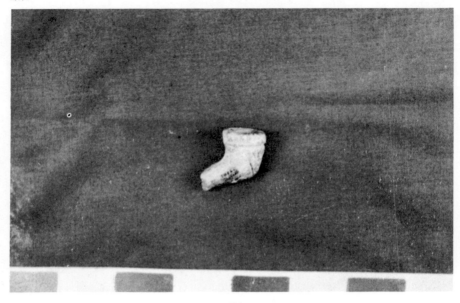

(b)

PART III.
CONCLUSIONS

By focusing on smoking technology, I hope I have provided new insights into the culture history of the aborigines of the Iroquois area. Hopefully, my inclusion of ethnohistorical data in what might be classified as a predominantly archaeological paper has been justified and enlightening. In presenting the archaeological data, my aim has consistently been the presentation of a meaningful and analytically useful typology, organized by acceptable and workable criteria and evaluated both archaeologically and geographically.

My relative success in achieving my goals may perhaps be judged best by examination of my data as presented in Tables 4 and 5, which show the archaeological and geographical breakdown of all the pipes I examined personally before I compiled the typology (still, of course, in accordance with Ritchie's schemes, to which I have adhered through-out for reasons stated in my introduction to Part II). Altogether I drew and recorded 661 artifacts for this project. Of this number, 193 could be identified only by county; 54 were classified only as originating from sites within New York State. Many others that I examined in private and museum collections, but to which I do not refer in my study, were totally without provenience data. I shall not evaluate the completeness of data in the individual museum collections, for, with some variation, the provenience data improved generally for artifacts from recently, and professionally, excavated sites.

Table 4 lists 226 pipes and tubes that have originated from sites identifiable by culture. This number may not be large enough for valid statistical analysis, but, hopefully, it is a sufficient sample to show broad trends. In Table 5 I have listed by type the provenience of all 376 New York State pipes whose counties of origin are known. I have also listed as "unknown" the 54 artifacts for which no provenience other than New York State was given, and I have included, for comparison, those 231 pipes I examined from Ontario, Canada. I have not recorded dateless pipes merely purported to have originated in the area studied. They constituted quite a large number, and each, unfortunately, represents a loss of our potential knowledge of the history of the people in this area.

My most important conclusion from these data is that correlations seem to exist between the construction and style of artifacts and the sites in which they were found—that is, artifacts of a given type tend to cluster in a given geographical area and occur in sites attributed to a certain archaeological culture. An unusually good example is the ring-bowl clay pipe in New York. Of 44 New York ring-bowl pipes seen, 34 were from sites in the Central Subarea. Of 31 ring-bowl pipes

231

classifiable by culture, 30, or 96.8 percent, were Iroquoian. Again, we must remember that the sample may be biased toward the Central Subarea; however, my findings at least indicate that the sample of artifacts I used was fairly diagnostic of the range of pipe styles manufactured by the tribes under investigation.

The data in Table 4 seem to corroborate my hypothesis that the typology, in the general order in which I have presented it, may reflect a chronological progression in time. For example, the first two stone pipes—the block-end tube and the plain-bore tube—are also apparently the oldest, both generally attributed in the literature to the Early Woodland Culture. The greater number of clay pipes examined perhaps offers a broader base upon which to hypothesize this, as well as other, general trends. For example, the discrete-chambered tube is apparently a Point Peninsula artifact (a shaky guess after seeing only two examples, but corroborated in the literature). The more complex simple obtuse-angle and basket-bowl pipes are apparently Owasco artifacts, with 61.3 percent and 85.7 percent, respectively, of the total artifacts attributable to a culture designated as Owasco. The even more complex clay pipes that follow the basket-bowl pipe in the typology are apparently Iroquoian artifacts, as the following data from Table 4 indicate: ring bowl, 96.8 percent Iroquoian; trumpet, 80 percent; square collared, 100 percent; escutcheon, 100 percent; human effigy, 95 percent; mammal, bird, open-mouth, and reptile and amphibian effigies, 100 percent; and miscellaneous obtuse-angle, 100 percent.

It is also significant that the numbers of artifacts increase in each successive culture. This factor may result from researchers unearthing recent sites more often than old sites. Also, the more recent artifacts might be less likely to have deteriorated or to have been destroyed owing to their relatively shorter interment. Then, too, I feel that the fact cannot but reflect the inception and growth of a more sedentary and argicultural society. During the Owasco and final Iroquoian Cultures, this cultural change is visible in the aborigines' ever more skillful manipulation and utilization of their raw materials—for example, clay in pottery smoking pipes.

Table 5 shows a heavy geographical distribution in the Central and Northern Subareas of New York State and in the Neutral area of Ontario, Canada. These data correspond to the concentration of Iroquoian occupation, but are probably more indicative of the range of artifacts in the collections I studied. Only one pipe distribution would lead me to hypothesize that the type might well be an exclusive local design. Of 13 escutcheon pipes examined, 100 percent were from sites in the Northern Subarea attributed to the Iroquoian Culture.

Certainly one of my most important discoveries in my research for this study has been that private and museum collections, although often poorly documented, can be useful as analytical tools in formulating typologies. The earth does not contain an unlimited supply of artifacts, and these aggregations will become increasingly valuable as the undiscovered material supply decreases. It is the job of the museum and private collector to disseminate data regarding their collections and to make them available for study, and it is the duty of the student to use them wisely.

TABLE 4. Pipe Typology Classified by Culture*

Type	Culture				
	Early Woodland	Point Peninsula	Owasco	Iroquoian	Total
STONE: Block-end tube	75.0 3 100.0				3 100.0
Plain-bore tube	25.0 1 100.0				1 100.0
Platform, curved base					
Platform, straight base					
Obtuse angle			2.2 1 50.0	.5 1 50.0	2 100.0
Boulder				1.2 2 100.0	2 100.0
Vasiform			2.2 1 16.7	3.0 5 83.3	6 100.0
Keel base				3.0 5 100.0	5 100.0
Calumet				1.8 3 100.0	3 100.0
Miscellaneous			2.2 1 20.0	2.4 4 80.0	5 100.0
CLAY:† Discrete-chambered tube		20.0 2 100.0			2 100.0
Simple obtuse angle		70.0 7 22.6	42.2 19 61.3	3.0 5 16.1	31 100.0
Basket bowl			40.0 18 85.7	1.8 3 14.3	21 100.0
Ring bowl		10.0 1 3.2		18.0 30 96.8	31 100.0
Trumpet			9.2 4 20.0	9.6 16 80.0	20 100.0

TABLE 4 (cont.)

Type	Culture				
	Early Woodland	Point Peninsula	Owasco	Iroquoian	Total
Square collared				3.6 6 100.0	6 100.0
Escutcheon				7.8 13 100.0	13 100.0
Human effigy			2.2 1 5.3	10.8 18 94.7	19 100.0
Mammal Effigy				4.8 8 100.0	8 100.0
Bird effigy				5.4 9 100.0	9 100.0
Open-mouth effigy				3.0 5 100.0	5 100.0
Reptile and amphibian effigy				1.8 3 100.0	3 100.0
Miscellaneous				18.6 31 100.0	31 100.0
Total	100.0 4	100.0 10	100.0 45	100.0 167	226

* The number in the center of each box represents the number of artifacts of the given type from the given culture that I actually examined. The figure in the upper left-hand corner, reading from top to bottom, represents the percentage that that type is of all the artifacts attributed to that culture. The figure in the lower right-hand corner, reading from left to right, represents the percentage of the total number of pipes of that type that is attributed to that culture. For example, 75 percent of all the artifacts from the Adenalike Culture that I examined personally were block-end stone tubes, and 100 percent of all the block-end stone tubes that I studied were attributed to the Adenalike Culture.

† Inasmuch as my information regarding the plain-bore clay tube was mostly from the literature, the type does not appear in my data evaluations, although I have included it in my typology.

TABLE 5. Pipe Typology Classified by Subcultural Areas*

Type	New York State							Ontario, Canada		Total
	Western	Central	Northern	Eastern	Southern	Unknown	Neutral	Huronia	Saint Lawrence	
STONE: Block-end tube		.5 1 25.0	.9 1 25.0	5.3 1 25.0		1.9 1 25.0				4 100.0
Plain-bore tube	2.6 1 14.3	2.0 4 57.1		5.3 1 14.3	14.3 1 14.3					7 100.0
Platform, curved base			.9 1 50.0	5.3 1 50.0						2 100.0
Platform, straight base	2.6 1 7.7	2.5 5 38.5	.9 1 7.7	5.3 1 7.7	14.3 1 7.7	1.9 1 7.7	1.4 3 23.1			13 100.0
Obtuse angle	2.6 1 7.7	1.5 3 23.1	2.7 3 23.1				2.8 6 46.2			13 100.0
Boulder	7.7 3 50.0	1.0 2 33.3						8.3 1 16.7		6 100.0
Vasiform	2.6 1 2.7	6.5 13 35.1	.9 1 2.7	10.5 2 5.4			7.9 17 45.9	8.3 1 2.7	40.00 2 5.4	37 100.0
Keel base		6.0 12 52.2	.9 1 4.3				3.7 8 34.8	8.3 1 4.3	20.0 1 4.3	23 100.0
Calumet	5.1 2 12.5	1.5 3 18.8		5.3 1 6.3			4.7 10 62.5			16 100.0
Miscellaneous	5.1 2 8.3	6.5 13 54.2	3.6 4 16.7	5.3 1 4.2			1.9 4 16.7			24 100.0

TABLE 5 (cont.)

Type	New York State						Ontario, Canada			Total
	Western	Central	Northern	Eastern	Southern	Unknown	Neutral	Huronia	Saint Lawrence	
CLAY:† Discrete-chambered tube		1.0 / 2 / 66.7				1.9 / 1 / 33.3				3 / 100.0
Simple obtuse angle	2.6 / 1 / 1.8	14.4 / 29 / 50.9	7.3 / 8 / 14.0			11.1 / 6 / 10.5	5.6 / 12 / 21.1		20.0 / 1 / 1.8	57 / 100.0
Basket bowl		10.5 / 21 / 91.4	.9 / 1 / 4.3			1.9 / 1 / 4.3				23 / 100.0
Ring bowl	12.9 / 5 / 4.9	16.9 / 34 / 33.3	.9 / 1 / 1.0	5.3 / 1 / 1.0	14.3 / 1 / 1.0	3.7 / 2 / 2.0	26.2 / 56 / 54.9	8.3 / 1 / 1.0	20.0 / 1 / 1.0	102 / 100.0
Trumpet	15.4 / 6 / 5.8	5.0 / 10 / 9.7	25.5 / 28 / 27.9	15.8 / 3 / 2.9		7.4 / 4 / 3.8	22.4 / 48 / 46.6	33.3 / 4 / 3.9		103 / 100.0
Square collared	7.7 / 3 / 10.3	2.0 / 4 / 13.8	6.4 / 7 / 24.1		14.3 / 1 / 3.4		6.1 / 13 / 44.8	8.3 / 1 / 3.4		29 / 100.0
Escutcheon			11.8 / 13 / 100.0							13 / 100.0
Human effigy		5.5 / 11 / 23.9	10.9 / 12 / 26.1	5.3 / 1 / 2.2		3.7 / 2 / 4.3	8.4 / 18 / 39.1	16.7 / 2 / 4.3		46 / 100.0
Mammal effigy	5.1 / 2 / 7.4	5.0 / 10 / 37.0	.9 / 1 / 3.7	5.3 / 1 / 3.7	14.3 / 1 / 3.7	1.9 / 1 / 3.7	4.7 / 10 / 37.0	8.3 / 1 / 3.7		27 / 100.0
Bird effigy	5.1 / 2 / 11.1	2.0 / 4 / 22.2	3.6 / 4 / 22.2	15.8 / 3 / 16.7		1.9 / 1 / 5.6	1.9 / 4 / 22.2			18 / 100.0

TABLE 5 (cont.)

Type	New York State						Ontario, Canada			Total
	Western	Central	Northern	Eastern	Southern	Unknown	Neutral	Huronia	Saint Lawrence	
Open-mouth effigy	5.1 / 2 / 25.0	.5 / 1 / 12.5	1.8 / 2 / 25.0			1.9 / 1 / 12.5	.9 / 2 / 25.0			8 / 100.0
Reptile and amphibian effigy	2.6 / 1 / 10.0	.5 / 1 / 10.0	2.7 / 3 / 30.0			3.7 / 2 / 20.0	1.4 / 3 / 30.0			10 / 100.0
Miscellaneous	15.4 / 6 / 7.8	9.0 / 18 / 23.4	16.4 / 18 / 23.4	10.5 / 2 / 2.6	28.6 / 2 / 2.6	57.4 / 31 / 40.3				77 / 100.0
Total	100.0 / 39	100.0 / 201	100.0 / 110	100.0 / 19	100.0 / 7	100.0 / 54	100.0 / 214	100.0 / 12	100.0 / 5	661

* The number in the center of each box represents the number of artifacts of the given type from the given area that I actually examined. The figure in the upper left-hand corner, reading from top to bottom, represents the percentage that that type is of all the artifacts found in that area. The figure in the lower right-hand corner, reading from left to right, represents the percentage of the total number of pipes of that type that is found in that area. For example, 0.5 percent of all the artifacts from the Central Subarea that I examined personally were block-end stone tubes, and 25 percent of all the block-end stone tubes that I studied were found in the Central Subarea.

† Inasmuch as my information regarding the plain-bore clay tube was mostly from the literature, the type does not appear in my data evaluations, although I have included it in my typology.

BIBLIOGRAPHY

Akweks, Aren
  1951   *The Great Gift, Tobacco.* Akwesasne Counselor Organiza-
            tion, St. Regis Mohawk Reservation, Hogansburg, N. Y.

Arents, George
  1939   *The Seed from which Virginia Grew.* Address made at the
            College of William and Mary on the occasion of the Charter
            Day Exercises, Feb. 8, 1939. Williamsburg, Va.

Bailey, L. H. (editor)
  1935   *The Standard Cyclopedia of Horticulture.* 3 Vols. The
            Macmillan Company, New York.

Barber, Edwin A.
  1883   Catlinite. *American Naturalist,* Vol. 17, Part 2, pp. 745–
            64. Philadelphia.

Beauchamp, William M.
  1889   Indian Tobacco. Notes and Queries, *The Journal of Ameri-
            can Folk-Lore,* Vol. 2, No. 6, p. 234. New York.

  1897   Polished Stone Articles Used by the New York Aborigines.
            Bulletin of the New York State Museum, Vol. 4, No. 18.
            Albany.

  1902   Metallic Implements of the New York Indians. *New York
            State Museum Bulletin No. 55.* Albany.

  1907   Civil Religious and Mourning Councils and Ceremonies
            of Adoption of the New York Indians. *New York State Mu-
            seum Bulletin No. 113,* pp. 341–451. Albany.

Berlin, Alfred Franklin
  1905   Early Smoking Pipes of the North American Aborigines.
            *Proceedings and Collections of the Wyoming Historical
            and Geological Society for the Year 1905,* Vol. 9, pp. 107–
            36. Wilkes-Barre, Pa.

Blair, Helen Emma (editor)
  1911   *The Indian Tribes of the Upper Mississippi Valley and
            Region of the Great Lakes.* Vol. 1 of 2 Vols. Arthur H.
            Clark Co., Cleveland, Ohio.

Blau, Harold
  1964   The Iroquois White Dog Sacrifice: Its Evolution and
            Symbolism. *Ethnohistory,* Vol. 2, No. 2, pp. 97–119. Bloom-
            ington, Ind.

Chittenden, Frederick J. (editor)
  1956   *Dictionary of Gardening.* 2nd ed., Vol. 3. Oxford at the
            Clarendon Press.

Crane, H. R.
  1956   University of Michigan Radiocarbon Dates I. *Science,* Vol.
            124, No. 3224, pp. 664–72. Washington, D. C.

Dana, Mrs. William Starr
    1910   *How To Know the Wild Flowers*. Charles Scribner's Sons,
            New York.

Dixon, Roland B., and Stetson, John B., Jr.
    1922   Analysis of Pre-Columbian Pipe Dottels. *American Anthro-
            pologist*, Vol. 24, No. 2, pp. 245–46. Menasha, Wis.

Douglas, Jordan
    1959   Adena and Blocked-End Tubes in the Northeast. *Bulletin
            of the Massachusetts Archaeological Society*, Vol. 20, No. 4,
            pp. 49–61. Attleboro.

Driver, Harold E.
    1964   *Indians of North America*. University of Chicago Press,
            Chicago.

Drumm, Judith
    1962   *Iroquois Culture. Educational Leaflet No. 5*, State Museum
            and Science Service, Albany.

Dunhill, Alfred
    1924   *The Pipe Book*. A. & C. Black, Ltd., London, England.

Fenton, William N.
    1940   Problems Arising from the Historic Northeastern Position
            of the Iroquois. *Essays in Historical Anthropology of North
            America*. Reprinted from the *Smithsonian Miscellaneous
            Collections*, Vol. 100, pp. 159–251. Washington, D. C.

    1942   Contacts Between Iroquois Herbalism and Colonial Medi-
            cine. *Annual Report of the Smithsonian Institution, 1941*,
            pp. 503–26. Washington, D. C.

    1953   The Iroquois Eagle Dance, An Offshoot of the Calumet
            Dance. *Smithsonian Institution Bureau of American Eth-
            nology Bulletin 156*. Washington, D. C.

Fowler, William S.
    1951   Pipes and Rare Products of the Stone Bowl Industry. *Bulle-
            tin of the Massachusetts Archaeological Society*, Vol. 13, No.
            1, pp. 13–20. Attleboro.

Gleason, Henry A.
    1952   *New Britin and Brown's Illustrated Flora of the North-
            eastern United States*, Vol. 3. New York Botanical Gardens
            and Lancaster Press, Lancaster, Pa.

Griffin, James B.
    1961   Review of *The Eastern Dispersal of the Adena*, by Ritchie
            and Dragoo. *American Antiquity*, Vol. 26, No. 4, p. 572.
            Washington, D. C.

Guthe, Alfred K.
    1958   The Late Prehistoric Occupation in Southwestern New
            York: An Interpretive Analysis. *Research Records of the
            Rochester Museum of Arts and Sciences No. 11*. Rochester.

Hale, Horatio
    1885   The Iroquois Sacrifice of the White Dog. *The American
            Antiquarian and Oriental Journal*, Vol. 7, No. 1, pp. 7–14.
            Chicago.

Hall, Edward Hagaman
    1910   Henry Hudson and the Discovery of the Hudson River;

Chapter XI Juet's Journal of the Voyages of the Half Moon. Being appendix B in the *Fifteenth Annual Report of the American Scenic and Historic Preservation Society*, pp. 308–46. Albany.

Harrington, Mark Raymond
 1922 A Midcolonial Site in Erie County. *The Archaeological History of New York, Part I*, ed. by A. C. Parker, *New York State Museum Bulletins 235* and *236*, pp. 207–237. Albany.

 1965 *The Iroquois Trail.* Rutgers University Press, New Brunswick, N. J.

Hayes, Charles F., III
 1965 The Orringh Stone Tavern and Three Seneca Sites of the Late Historic Period. *Research Records of the Rochester Museum of Arts and Sciences No. 12.* Rochester.

Hegi, Philip G.
 n.d. *Illustriertie Flora von Mittel Europa.* München, Deutschland.

Hewitt, J. N. B.
 1907 Calumet. In *Handbook of American Indians North of Mexico,* ed. by F. W. Hodge. *Smithsonian Institution Bureau of American Ethnology Bulletin 30,* Vol. 1 of 2 Vols., pp. 191–95. Washington, D. C.

Hill, Roland B. (editor)
 1953 *Orite of Adequantega: The Journal of Johannes van Dyk, 1634–1635.* The Reporter Company, Inc., Walton, N. Y.

Hodge, Frederick Webb (editor)
 1907 *Handbook of American Indians North of Mexico. Smithsonian Institution Bureau of American Ethnology Bulletin 30,* Vol. 1 of 2 Vols. Washington, D. C.

 1910 *Handbook of American Indians North of Mexico. Smithsonian Institution Bureau of American Ethnology Bulletin 30,* Vol. 2 of 2 Vols. Washington, D. C.

Hoffman, Albert J.
 1956 The McClintock Burial Site. *New York State Archaeological Association Bulletin No. 7,* pp. 3–5.

Hunt, George T.
 1940 *The Wars of the Iroquois, A Study in Intertribal Trade Relations.* University of Wisconsin Press, Madison, Wis.

Kell, Katherine T.
 1965 Tobacco in Folk Cures in Western Society. *Journal of American Folklore,* Vol. 78, No. 308, pp. 99–114. Richmond, Va.

Keppler, Joseph
 1941 *Comments on Certain Iroquois Masks. Contributions from the Museum of the American Indian, Heye Foundation,* Vol. 12, No. 4. New York.

Lenig, Donald
 1965 The Oak Hill Horizon and Its Relation to the Development of Five Nations Iroquois Culture. *Researches and Transactions of the New York State Archaeological Association,* Vol. 15, No. 1. Buffalo.

Linton, Ralph
    1924   Use of Tobacco Among North American Indians. *Field Museum of Natural History Anthropology Leaflet No. 15.* Chicago.

Lorenz, Konrad
    1966   *On Aggression,* trans. by Marjorie Kerr Wilson. Harcourt, Brace and World, Inc., New York.

MacNeish, Richard S.
    1952   Iroquois Pottery Types, A Technique for the Study of Iroquois Prehistory. *National Museum of Canada Bulletin 124.* Ottawa, Canada.

Mooney, James, and Olbrechts, Frans M.
    1932   *The Swimmer Manuscript: Cherokee Sacred Formulas and Medicinal Prescriptions. Smithsonian Institution Bureau of American Ethnology Bulletin 99.* Washington, D. C.

Morgan, Richard G.
    1952   Outline of Cultures in the Ohio Region. *Archaeology of the Eastern United States,* ed. by James B. Griffin, pp. 83–98. University of Chicago Press, Chicago.

Murphy, Edith Van Allen
    1959   *Indian Uses of Native Plants.* Desert Printers, Inc., Palm Desert, Calif.

Nicholet, I. N.
    1841   Catlinite. *Senate Document 237,* 26th Congress, Second Session, 1840–1841.

Parker, Arthur C.
    1907   Excavations in an Erie Village and Burial Site at Ripley, Chautauqua County, New York. *New York State Museum Bulletin No. 117.* Albany.

    1922   *The Archaeological History of New York. New York State Museum Bulletins 235–36, Part 1,* and *237–38, Part 2.* Albany.

Parkman, Francis
    1880   *Pioneers of Old France in the New World, Part First.* Little, Brown and Company, Boston, Mass.

Peattie, Donald Culross
    1950   *A Natural History of Trees of Eastern and Central North America.* Houghton Mifflin Company, Boston, Mass.

Pendergast, James F.
    1966   *Three Prehistoric Iroquois Components in Eastern Ontario: The Salem, Gray's Creek, and Beckstead Sites. National Museum of Canada Bulletin No. 208, Anthropological Series No. 73.* Ottawa, Canada.

Philhower, Charles A. (editor)
    1934   Indian Pipes and the Use of Tobacco in New Jersey. *The Archaeological Society of New Jersey Leaflet No. 3.* Trenton.

Rand McNally New Cosmopolitan World Atlas
    1966   Rand McNally Co., New York.

Ritchie, William A.
    1936   A Prehistoric Fortified Village Site at Canandaigua, Ontario County, New York. *Research Records of the Rochester Museum of Arts and Sciences No. 3.* Rochester.

1937   Culture Influences from Ohio in New York Archaeology.
          American Antiquity, Vol. 2, No. 3, pp. 182–94. Menasha,
          Wis.

1938   Certain Recently Explored New York Mounds and Their
          Probable Relation to the Hopewell Culture. *Research Rec-
          ords of the Rochester Museum of Arts and Sciences No. 4.*
          Rochester.

1944   The Pre-Iroquoian Occupations of New York State. *Memoir
          No. 1*, Rochester Museum of Arts and Sciences. Rochester.

1952   The Chance Horizon, An Early Stage of Mohawk Iroquois
          Cultural Development. *New York State Museum, Circular
          29*, New York State Science Service. Albany.

1953   Indian History of New York State; Part I, Pre-Iroquoian
          Cultures. *Educational Leaflet No. 6*, rev., New York State
          Museum. Albany.

1954   Dutch Hollow, An Early Historic Period Seneca Site in
          Livingston County, New York. *Researches and Transac-
          tions of the New York State Archaeological Association*, Vol.
          13, No. 1. Albany. (Also *Research Records of the Rochester
          Museum of Arts and Sciences No. 10.*)

1955   Recent Discoveries Suggesting an Early Woodland Burial
          Cult in the Northeast. *New York State Museum and Science
          Service, Circular 40.* Albany.

1958   An Introduction to Hudson Valley Prehistory. *New York
          State Museum and Science Service Bulletin Number 367.*
          Albany.

1961   A Typology and Nomenclature for New York Projectile
          Points. *New York State Museum and Science Service Bul-
          letin Number 384.* Albany.

1965   *The Archaeology of New York State.* Natural History Press,
          Garden City, N. Y.

Ritchie, William A., and Dragoo, Donald W.
    1960   The Eastern Dispersal of Adena. *New York State Museum
              and Science Service Bulletin Number 379.* Albany.

Ritchie, William A., and MacNeish, Richard S.
    1949   The Pre-Iroquoian Pottery of New York State. *American
              Antiquity*, Vol. 15, No. 2, pp. 97–124. Menasha, Wis.

Ritchie, William A., Lenig, Donald P., and Miller, P. Schuyler
    1953   An Early Owasco Sequence in Eastern New York. *New York
              State Museum Circular 32.* Albany.

Ritzenthaler, Robert E.
    1955   Kinnikinnick. *Lore*, Vol. 6, No. 1, Milwaukee Public Mu-
              seum. Milwaukee, Wis.

Setchell, William Albert
    1921   Aboriginal Tobaccos. *American Anthropologist*, Vol. 23,
              No. 4, pp. 397–414. Lancaster, Pa.

Skinner, Alanson
    1921   Notes on Iroquois Archaeology. *Indian Notes and Mono-
              graphs*, Miscellaneous Series No. 18, ed. by F. W. Hodge.
              Museum of the American Indian, Heye Foundation, New
              York.

    1925   Some Seneca Tobacco Customs. *Indian Notes*, Vol. 2, No. 2,

        pp. 127–30. Museum of the American Indian, Heye Founda-
        tion, New York.

    1926   An Unusual Canadian Disc Pipe. *Indian Notes*, Vol. 3, No.
            1, pp. 39–41. Museum of the American Indian, Heye Foun-
            dation, New York.

Smith, De Cost
    1888   Witchcraft and Demonism of the Modern Iroquois. *Journal
            of American Folk-Lore*, Vol. 1, No. 3, pp. 184–93. Boston.

    1889A   Additional Notes on Onondaga Witchcraft and Hoⁿ-do'-I.
            Journal of American Folk-Lore, Vol. 2, No. 7, pp. 277–81.
            Boston.

    1889B   Onondaga Superstitions. *Journal of American Folk-Lore*,
            Vol. 2, No. 7, pp. 282–83. Boston.

Smith, John   (Capt.)
    1819   *The True Travels, Adventures and Observations of Cap-
            taine John Smith, in Europe, Asia, Africke, and America.*
            Vol. 1. From the London edition of 1629, republished at
            the Franklin Press by William W. Gray, Printer, Rich-
            mond, Va.

Thwaites, Reuben G.   (editor)
    1901   *The Jesuit Relations and Allied Documents.* 73 Vols. Cleve-
            land, Ohio.

Trelease, Alan W.
    1960   *Indian Affairs in Colonial New York: The Seventeenth
            Century.* Cornell University Press, Ithaca, N. Y.

West, George Arbor
    1934   Tobacco, Pipes and Smoking Customs of the American
            Indians, Parts I and II. *Bulletin of the Public Museum of
            the City of Milwaukee*, Vol. 17. Milwaukee, Wis.

White, Marian E.
    1956   Morgan Chapter Dig. *New York State Archaeological Asso-
            ciation Bulletin No. 7*, pp. 13–14. Rochester.

    1961   Iroquois Culture History in the Niagara Frontier Area of
            New York State. *Anthropological Papers No. 16*, Museum of
            Anthropology, University of Michigan. Ann Arbor.

Wiener, Leo
    1925   The Philological History of "Tobacco" in America. Vol. 1.
            XXIe Congrès international des Americanistes, 1924, pp.
            305–14. Göteborg.

Witthoft, John, Schoff, Harry L., and Wray, Charles Foster
    1953   Micmac Pipes, Vase-Shaped Pipes, and Calumets. *Pennsyl-
            vania Archaeologist*, Vol. 23, Nos. 3–4, pp. 89–107.

Wray, Charles Foster
    1956A   Seneca Tobacco Pipes. *New York State Archaeological Asso-
            ciation Bulletin No. 6*, pp. 15–16. Rochester.

    1956B   Archaeological Evidence of the Mask Among the Seneca.
            New York State Archaeological Association Bulletin No. 7,
            pp. 7–8. Rochester.

Wray, Charles Foster, and Graham, Robert John
    1966   The Boughton Hill site, Victor, New York. Unpublished
            paper, presented at the Annual Meeting of the New York

State Archaeological Association, held at the Rochester Museum of Arts and Sciences, Saturday, April 23, 1966. (Mimeograph copies available.)

Wray, Charles Foster, and Schoff, Harry L.
  1953   A Preliminary Report on the Seneca Sequence in Western New York, 1550–1687. *Pennsylvania Archaeologist,* Vol. 23, No. 2, pp. 53–63.

Yarnell, Richard Asa
  1964   Aboriginal Relationships Between Culture and Plant Life in the Upper Great Lakes Region. *Anthropological Papers, No. 23.* Museum of Anthropology, University of Michigan, Ann Arbor.

INDEX

Abnaki, 95
aboriginal linguistic groups, 13
aboriginal tobacco use, 19–21, 24–28
Adams Center site, 41, 43
Adams site, 86
Adena Culture, 40, 52–53, 108, 235
Albany County, 38
Algonquian Indians, 13, 19
Algonquian language stock, 13, 31
Algonquian peoples, 37
Algonquin ceremonies, 20
Allegany County, 25, 38
Amber site, 42, 43
amphibian effigy. See pipes
animal oil, 32
archaeological reports, 35–220
archaeological sites, alphabetical list, 43–
  47; bibliographical data, 43–47; by cul-
  ture and subarea, 41–42; in New Jersey,
  43; in Pennsylvania, 86
Archaic Period, 37
arrow root, 31
Aurora site, 41, 43

Bainbridge site, 42, 43
bar base calumet. See pipes
basket bowl. See pipes
Bell-Philhower site, 43, 112
Bettysburg site, 77
Big Salmon Creek site, 41, 43
Big Tree Farm site, 41, 42, 43, 76
bird effigy. See pipes
black birch, 32
Black River site, 41, 43, 77, 158
block-end tube. See pipes
"blood" diseases, 28
Boughton Hill site, 41, 43, 142, 144, 150,
  155, 181, 193, 199, 204, 218
boulder. See pipe
bowl-base perforations, 103–4
Bradt site, 42, 43
Bringer of Rain, 26
Bronx County, 38
Brooklyn Botanical Gardens, 28
Broome County, 38, 43, 47, 83

Buffam Street site, 41, 43, 211
burning bush, 32
burning-of-the-white-dog ceremony, 25
Burning Springs site, 41, 43, 130

Caine Mound site, 76
Calcium site, 41, 43
calicobush, 31
Calligan Farm site, 41, 43, 153, 188
calumet pipe. See pipe
calumet ritual, 20, 94, 105; as "displace-
  ment activity," 23; diffusion of, 21, 22–23,
  24; symbolism of, 20, 21
Camillus site, 42, 43, 61
Canandaigua Lake, 97
Canandaigua site, 42, 43
Canawaugus site, 41, 43
Canton Appenzell, 103, 104
carbon dating, 40
Castle Creek site, 42, 43
catlinite, 94, 104–5
Cattaraugus County, 38, 43, 44, 81, 130,
  196, 207
Cattaraugus Reservation, 81, 196, 207
Cayuga County, 38, 43, 44, 45, 46, 84, 92,
  112, 118, 120, 121, 125, 130, 138, 144, 147,
  148, 156, 166, 167, 180, 192, 196, 205
Cayugas, 28, 29
Cayuga tribal area, 12
Champlain, 19
Charlesvoix, 21
Chautauqua County, 38, 44, 45, 46, 47, 146
chemical analyses, of pipe dottle, 32–33
Chemung County, 38
Chenango County, 38, 43, 66, 72, 77, 112,
  116, 133, 137
Cherokee medicine men, 25
cherry bark, 32
Chesapeake Bay, 19
Chippewa, dialect, 31
Clinton County, 38
Cold Spring Reservation, 25
Columbia County, 38, 68
copper, used in pipes, 19
Cornish site, 41, 44

247